PASSPORT
ISRAEL

110669597

WITHDRAWN

Passport to the World

Passport Argentina
Passport Brazil
Passport China
Passport France
Passport Germany
Passport Hong Kong
Passport India
Passport Italy
Passport Japan
Passport Korea
Passport Malaysia
Passport Mexico
Passport Philippines
Passport Russia
Passport Singapore
Passport South Africa
Passport Spain
Passport Taiwan
Passport Thailand
Passport United Kingdom
Passport USA
Passport Vietnam

PASSPORT
ISRAEL

Your Pocket Guide
to
Israeli Business,
Customs & Etiquette

Donna Rosenthal

Passport Series Editor: Barbara Szerlip

WORLD TRADE PRESS®
Professional Books for International Trade

World Trade Press
1505 Fifth Avenue
San Rafael, California 94901 USA
Tel: (415) 454-9934
Fax: (415) 453-7980
USA Order Line: (800) 833-8586
E-mail: WorldPress@aol.com

"Passport to the World" concept: Edward Hinkelman
Cover and book design: Peter Jones
Illustrations: Tom Watson
Cover photography courtesy of Israel Ministry of Tourism

THIS PUBLICATION IS DESIGNED TO PROVIDE GENERAL
INFORMATION CONCERNING THE CULTURAL ASPECTS OF
DOING BUSINESS WITH PEOPLE FROM A PARTICULAR COUN-
TRY. IT IS SOLD WITH THE UNDERSTANDING THAT THE PUB-
LISHER IS NOT ENGAGED IN RENDERING LEGAL OR ANY
OTHER PROFESSIONAL SERVICES. IF LEGAL ADVICE OR OTHER
EXPERT ASSISTANCE IS REQUIRED, THE SERVICES OF A COM-
PETENT PROFESSIONAL PERSON SHOULD BE SOUGHT.

Library of Congress Cataloging-in-Publication Data
Rosenthal, Donna, 1950 –
Passport Israel: your pocket guide to Israeli business, customs & etiquette
/ Donna Rosenthal.
p. cm. -- (Passport to the world)
ISBN 1-885073-22-4 (pbk.)
1. Corporate culture--Israel. 2. Business etiquette--Israel.
3. Negotiation in business--Israel. 4. Intercultural communication.
I. Title. II. Series.
HD58.7.R67 1996
390'.0095694--dc20
96-28183
CIP

Printed in the United States of America

Israel

The Promised Land

1 Doing Business Across Cultures

Although business operations around the world are becoming standardized, national traditions, attitudes and beliefs remain diverse. While Americans and Europeans tend to enjoy public praise, for example, it may be a source of embarrassment for a Japanese. This difference is based on the fact that some Western cultures value individuality of thought and action, while Eastern cultures often prize modesty and group consensus.

While the primary focus of people in one culture might be to get down to business quickly, another culture concentrates first on developing personal relationships. Although their objectives may be the same, people from different cultures are likely to have very different ways of achieving them.

You'll probably never know a particular culture as well as your own — not only is the language different, but the historical context within which its people operate is often misunderstood by outsiders.

Comparing Values Across Cultures

One Culture:	Another Culture:
Values change	Values tradition
Favors specific communication	Favors ambiguous communication
Values analytical, linear problem solving	Values intuitive, lateral problem solving
Places emphasis on individual performance	Places emphasis on group performance
Considers verbal communication most important	Considers context & nonverbal communication most important
Focuses on task and product	Focuses on relationship and process
Places emphasis on promoting differing views	Places emphasis on harmony and consensus
Emphasizes competition	Emphasizes collaboration
Prefers informal tone	Prefers formal tone
Is flexible about schedules	Emphasizes rigid adherence to schedule

Passport Israel will offer some insights into the country and its people and help you understand how local traditions, etiquette, values and communication styles differ from your own.

World Trade Press

Israel
Quick Look

Official name	Israel
Land area	21,501 sq km
Capital & largest city	Jerusalem (government center)
	Tel Aviv (business center)
Elevations	Highest–Mt. Hermon, 2,814 m.
	Lowest–Dead Sea, 400 m.
	below sea level (nearly 1/4
	mile, lowest point on earth)

People

Population (1995)	5.46 million
Density	280 people per sq. km.
Distribution	Over 90% urban
Annual growth (1996)	3%
Official languages	Hebrew and Arabic
Major religions	Judaism, Islam

Economy (1995)

GDP	US$86 billion
	US$15,650 per capita
Foreign trade	Imports—US$23,776
	Exports—US$16,884
Principal trade partners	U.S. US$4.272 billion
	E.U. US$14.803 billion
Currency	New Israeli Shekel (NIS)
	1 NIS = 100 agorot
Exchange Rate (8/96)	NIS1 = US$.317

Education and health

Literacy (1995)	95%
Universities	7
Medical Care	World's highest number of
	doctors per capita
Life expectancy (1995)	Women—78 years
	Men—75 years
Infant mortality (1995)	7.8 per 1,000 live births

ISRAEL

2 Country Facts

Tiny Land with a Long History

Israel is a sliver of land at the crossroad of three continents — Asia, Africa and Europe — and it's constantly facing the dilemmas of its geography. Surrounded by Lebanon, Syria, Jordan, Egypt and the new Palestinian Authority, Israel has never known permanent boundaries. Like its people, the land is a crazy quilt. There's the stunning Mediterranean coast, the reclaimed lush valleys and rolling hills of the Galilee, the rugged Negev desert and the coral reefs of the Red Sea.

History is visible everywhere. Jerusalem, the 3,000-year-old capital, is sacred to three religions. Within the walls of the Old City are the Western (Wailing) Wall, the Dome of the Rock mosque and the Church of the Holy Sepulcher. There are the mineral spas of the Dead Sea, the Biblical town of Nazareth, and ancient Jewish holy cities of Safad and Tiberias on Kinneret (Sea of Galilee), Israel's largest lake. Mountains, plains and desert are often minutes apart. Jerusalem is only a 45-minute drive from the skyscrapers and cafes of Tel Aviv (less, if you drive like an Israeli.)

Few areas in the world have been so fought over.

Assyrians, Babylonians, Persians, Greeks, Romans, Byzantines, Arabs and the Crusaders have all conquered the land. Looking at Israel today, it's hard to believe that for four centuries it was a semi-barren province of the Ottoman Turks until 1917, when British forces ousted them and the Balfour Declaration recognized a Jewish national home in Palestine. (The history of the Jews, and their roots to the land, span over thirty-five centuries.) Waves of Jewish immigrants arrived until 1939, when Arab anti-Jewish riots led Britain to cut off Jewish immigration. During World War II, with no refuge from Nazi persecution, two-thirds of Europe's Jews were murdered.

In 1947, after many pleas for statehood, the UN General Assembly adopted a resolution dividing the land into two states: one Jewish and one Arab. The United Nations recognized the State of Israel on May 14, 1948. Less than 24 hours later, the armies of Egypt, Jordan, Syria, Lebanon and Iraq invaded, fighting the severely outnumbered and under-equipped Israelis for 15 months. Over one percent of Israel's population died. The difficulty of life in the new state was reflected in former Prime Minister David Ben-Gurion's comment, "To be a realist here, you must believe in miracles."

Until recently, Israelis have lived in claustrophobic geographical and political isolation, surrounded by twenty-two hostile Arab states. The Peace Process of the 90s, however, is bringing new hope and increasing trade possibilities. The population has increased 57 percent in the last twenty years, and within the next thirty, Israel could become the world's most densely populated nation.

Climate

The climate ranges from temperate to sub-tropical, with plenty of sunshine. There are two distinct seasons: a mild, rainy winter from November through March and a warm, rainless season from April until mid-October. Regional conditions vary considerably. The coast has a Mediterranean climate that can be hot and humid. The hill regions have dry summers and moderately cold winters. The Negev has year-round semi-desert conditions. Average temperatures range from 5°C (41°F) in Jerusalem in the winter to over 40°C (95°F) in Eilat in midsummer.

Languages

Israelis are truly a polyglot people. Signs appear in the official languages of Hebrew and Arabic, as well as in English. There are 13 daily Hebrew newspapers and 11 others published in languages ranging from Russian to French and Arabic. *Kol Israel* (Voice of Israel) broadcasts radio programs in 17 languages.

Hebrew, the language of the Prophets and the Bible, is over 4,000 years old. Hebrew and Arabic (closely related Semitic languages) are both written from right to left. According to one theory, since the writing was originally carved in stone, a person holding a chisel in the left hand and the hammer in the right, had to make inscriptions from right to left in order to see the letters.

During the 2,000 years of exile, Hebrew served mostly as the language of liturgy, philosophy and literature. Eliezer Ben-Yehuda, creator of the first dictionary of modern Hebrew, was responsible for reviving Hebrew as a living, spoken language. After immigrating to Israel from Lithuania in 1881, Ben-Yehuda wanted the Jews to have a cultural rebirth. His son was the first child in centuries to speak Hebrew as his first language. Soon, Jewish immigrants from Eastern Europe who spoke Yiddish (an Eastern European Jewish language based on German and Hebrew) could communicate in Hebrew with local Palestinian Jews, who spoke Arabic or Ladino (medieval Spanish).

Modern Hebrew words had to be invented for things like telephones, tomatoes and taxi cabs. *Hashmal*, the Hebrew word for "electricity," for example, was taken from Ezekiel's vision of the heavens. Because Biblical Hebrew is bereft of colorful swear words, Israelis often borrow from Arabic; some Arabic words have also become Hebrew slang — such as *halas* (enough or finished), *yalla* (go ahead) and *shuk* (open-air market). Even though the Hebrew vocabulary has grown from some 8,000 words in Biblical times to over 120,000, a shepherd transported from Abraham's time could make himself understood today.

Business Hours

Sunday is the first day of the week. Most commercial offices are open Sunday through Thursday from 8 A.M. to 4 P.M. (and some from 8 A.M. to 1 P.M. Fridays). Business hours often depend on the city and type of business. Some shops close, Mediterranean style, for a lunch break and reopen in the late afternoon until about 7 P.M.

Israel uses three calendars, the Civil (Gregorian solar) for business purposes, the Hebrew lunar calendar of the Bible and the Moslem lunar calendar. Dates of Jewish holidays change each year, depending on the lunar cycle. Holidays always begin at dusk on the day before the holiday, with businesses shutting down in anticipation at 1 P.M.

Israeli Jewish offices are closed on these holidays:

Shabbat (Sabbath) .... Friday sundown to
Saturday sundown.

Rosh Hashanah ....Two days in September
(The New Year)   or October
Yom Kippur.................A holy fast, ten days after
(Day of Atonement)   Rosh Hashanah.
Succoth........................Four days after Yom Kippur
(Feast of the   for seven days. The first
Tabernacles)   and last days are holidays.
Pesah ....A week in Spring. The first
(Passover)   and last days are usually
                        holidays.
Israel Independence ..April or May
Day
Shavuot......................May or June.
(Festival of Weeks or
Harvest Festival)

Israeli Moslem offices are closed on these holidays:

Salah ....Friday afternoon prayers
                        (about noon on)
Id al- Fitr.....................Joyous feast day after the
                        month-long (daytime) fast
                        of Ramadan
Id al- Adha..................The day after the Hajj
(Feast of the Sacrifice) (pilgrimage to Mecca). It
                        commemorates God's com-
                        mand to Ibrahim to sacrifice
                        his son Ismail (Abraham
                        and Isaac in Jewish and
                        Christian traditions)

Israeli Arab Christians close their offices on
Christmas, Easter and New Year's Day.

(For more on these holidays, see Chapter 20:
Customs.)

The Israelis

A Salad Bowl of Peoples

Sitting in a noisy Tel Aviv sidewalk cafe, you'll see a kaleidoscope of Israelis. At the next table, two mini-skirted soldiers plan their post-military vacation to Bangkok. Nearby, an Egyptian-Israeli CD-ROM developer chats on his cellular phone. When a waitress serves him a cappuccino, her sleeve edges up, revealing numbers tattooed onto her arm — an indelible reminder of Auschwitz. At the next table, a Brazilian-Israeli architect with a ponytail proudly shows his designs to an Israeli-Ethiopian electrical engineer who grew up in a village without electricity. Just stand in line for an ATM or sun yourself on the beach and you'll overhear loud, heated discussions in over 70 different languages. About half of all Israelis are immigrants from more than 100 countries — from former Argentinians and Austrians to former Iraqis and Indians.

Dizzying Change

Israelis are passengers on a speeding roller coaster — racing up to elation, then down to despair. The velocity of recent events is astounding.

Yasser Arafat signed a peace agreement with the late Yitzak Rabin and Shimon Peres. So did King Hussein of Jordan (who later piloted his own helicopter from Amman to Tel Aviv). Jordanian soldiers are being treated in Tel Aviv hospitals, and a number of Arab states have opened diplomatic relations with Israel. After nearly five decades, international companies no longer shun Israel for fear of antagonizing oil-rich Arab countries. Israel has changed from a socialist economy into an export-oriented economy, a high-tech oasis and one of the fastest growing economies in the West. One out of seven Israelis has a cellular phone. Israeli television (forbidden until 1968 because it was deemed "uncivilized") now receives 45 cable stations from around the world — from BBC and Nightline to CNN and MTV. Israelis in Gap jeans and Reeboks prowl upscale malls hunting for McDonald's Golden Arches and Ben and Jerry's Ice Cream. "Dry Bones," a popular comic strip, puts it this way: "Cellular telephones? Pizza? Shopping malls? Cable TV? These days, the only way to tell if you're in America or the 'New Israel' is to go out for a walk after dark. If you don't get mugged, you're probably in Israel."

Into the '90s with a Vengeance

In 1995, *The Economist* placed Israel third (behind Singapore and Hong Kong) on the list of richest emerging economies. Highly educated Jews from the former Soviet Union are flooding in (nearly 700,000 of them since 1989). Quick converts to capitalism, they're buying apartments, cars and setting up high tech companies. The national bird seems to be the construction crane — marinas, malls, high rise offices, apartments and hotels are springing up everywhere. This is the end of Israel's socialist period, when the state owned the major industries. Capitalism is bringing the privatization of El Al Airlines and the sale of banks. High-tech multinationals, from Motorola to Microsoft, have set up shop. The "New Israel" is a Middle Eastern Silicon Valley wedded to innovative scientific, agricultural and medical research.

Between Iraq and The Hard Rock

The New Israel is a confusing mix of Bedouins and *Baywatch*, humus and the Hard Rock Cafe. Jerusalem's mall, the largest in the Middle East, has eight cinemas, some Jordanian and Egyptian shoppers, and the world's first kosher Burger King. Like their Arab neighbors, Israelis fancy *falafel* and shopping in *souks* (bustling open air markets filled with a vast array of spices and foods). About half of Israelis are Jews whose families immigrated from Moslem countries in the Middle East and North Africa. They grew up hearing Arabic, eating many of the same foods and enjoying the same musical rhythms as Israel's one million Arab citizens.

Like true Middle Easterners, Israelis stand close together, gesturing excitedly and arguing loudly as they bargain. The Yemenite-Israeli merchant who "caved in" and "gave" you "such a special deal" might invite you to sip mint tea and chat for an hour in the middle of the day. If you don't sit down and join him, he'll be insulted.

As the sun sets and the 3,000-year-old stones of Jerusalem turn pink in the dimming light, you can hear the *muezzin* calling the faithful to the mosque, church bells ringing, and Jews chanting ancient prayers in a synagogue. Here, as elsewhere in Israel, the past caresses the present.

Sometimes, however, the past smashes in. A fanatic Orthodox Jewish assassin's three bullets tried to kill the peace process. In a powerful gesture, Egypt's President Mubarak and Jordan's King Hussein came to Jerusalem to attend Prime Minister Yitzak Rabin's funeral. Palestinian Authority President Yassar Arafat comforted Rabin's widow in her home. As the Israeli roller coaster speeds on, alternating between pain and gain, the peace dividends lure investment and tourism to the Middle East. Regional integration and partnerships between Israeli and Arab companies are increasing. Is Israel a Jewish state in the Middle East or a Jewish Middle Eastern state?   Whatever the answer, Israel is part of a New Middle East.

"Why be happy? Worry."

Israelis invented this slogan. Until recently, Israel's borders were heavily guarded against its Arab neighbors. The only Hebrew-speaking Jewish country in the world, it was also culturally isolated. The Holocaust, during which six million Jews were killed in death camps, is still a part of living memory. Most Israelis believe that the Holocaust was possible because the Jews had no country of their own and no way to resist, and because the "civilized" world refused to help. Traumatic memories, coupled with Arab annihilation threats, contribute to Israeli toughness and resolve.

Because of its vulnerable location — 250 million Arabs surrounding 5.6 million Israelis in a country smaller than the U.S. state of New Jersey — Israelis are addicted to news reports. Israel has only half the population of New York City, but boasts five times as many daily newspapers. Radio news is played hourly (and loudly) in local buses, restaurants and offices. With news of new diplomatic relations with another Arab country, Israelis swing into euphoria. With news of another Hamas terrorist attack, they plunge into grief. Israel has suffered a geography of fear, but the peace process is creating a geography of hope. "Hope for the best and expect the worst" — this is the Israeli way of life.

More a Family Than a Country

When the worst does happen and a terrorist attack shatters lives, Israelis pull together. Each death is a shared personal tragedy in this tiny country, where everyone seems to know everyone else. Too many thousands of memorial candles have been lit, too many children's eyes are red from tears for parents or schoolmates killed by suicide bombers. Almost all Israelis have had loved ones killed in wars or terrorist attacks. Memorials to the dead dot the countryside. The small population adds to the heightened intensity of emotions and the strong sense of community. One of five Israelis (over a million) filed past Prime Minister Rabin's casket in Jerusalem — old and young, religious and secular, immigrant and native born. As one rabbi put it: "When one heart is torn open, all our hearts ache."

Israelis also celebrate together. When the radio announced the dramatic thirty-six hour airlift that brought 14,324 Ethiopian Jews from Addis Ababa to Tel Aviv in May 1991, both soldiers and bus drivers were crying. The country welcomed these Africans who, for centuries, had prayed in their mud synagogues to return to "The Promised Land." Since 1989, an avalanche of nearly 700,000 former Soviet Jews have also been welcomed. Israelis unflinching give all new immigrants huge subsidies. In turn, many newcomers are contributing greatly to Israel's burgeoning high-tech and bio-tech industries, as well as to its symphony orchestras.

A Multi-Cultural Mix

Pioneers, Refugees & Survivors

The "typical Israeli" doesn't exist; much depends on place of birth, cultural roots and whether he or she has studied or worked abroad. Most native-born Israelis are only one or two generations removed from an immigrant past.

The founders of the state were almost all *Ashkenazim* who fled persecution and poverty in Eastern Europe during the late 19th and early 20th centuries and immigrated to Palestine. (*Ashkenaz* is Hebrew for Germany.) These early pioneers called themselves Zionists, after Zion, the traditional synonym for Jerusalem and Israel. They believed that after two millennia in exile, Jews should return to their historic homeland. Many were social revolutionaries who tried to create a utopian, egalitarian, socialist society, religious but open to intellectual inquiry, with a focus on the group, not the individual. They drained malarial swamps and founded agricultural settlements. They had deep social passions and dreams, but life was difficult — there were suicides, mental anguish, weeping at night. As the country's first President, Chaim Weizmann once said: "To be a Zionist, it's not necessary to be mad, but it helps."

Those Jews had a strong influence on today's Israelis. Through hard physical labor, they tried to create a new Jew, different from the frightened, persecuted East European Jew. They took Hebrew names like *Barak* (lightning), *Tamir* (towering) and *Oz* (strength), or agricultural names like *Karmi* (of the vineyard) and *Dagan* (corn). They deliberately ate plain food, prepared in communal workers' kitchens. They were anti-authoritarian, straight-speaking and passionately informal. They hated jackets and dresses, and banned neckties as the symbols of the hypocritical, decadent Europe they had fled. They discouraged differences in income or rank. Eventually, these socialistic idealists evolved into the pragmatic realists who shaped pre-state Israel — realists like David Ben-Gurion and Golda Meir.

Sephardim & Jews From Moslem Lands

Between 1947 and 1952, Israel took in about 700,000 Jewish refugees who had fled North African and Middle Eastern countries that their families had lived in for centuries. Although they're collectively referred to as *Sephardim,* the term actually refers to the descendants of Jews who were expelled for their religious beliefs from Spain and Portugal at the end of the 15th Century. (*Sepharad* is Hebrew for Spain.) Many Sephardic Israelis still speak *Ladino* (medieval Spanish). The cultural differences between Sephardic Jews from Damascus, Rabat, Baghdad and Cairo are as great as those between Ashkenazi Jews from Paris, Prague and Pittsburgh.

Some Sephardim resent seeing Ashkenazim so heavily represented in the government, the universities and white-collar jobs. Gradually, however, Sephardim have been gaining a hold in Israel's political, economic, military, religious and cultural institutions, and distinctions are beginning to blur. Nearly a third of Israeli marriages today are "mixed" — Ashkenazi and Sephardi.

Sabras

Over half of Israeli Jews are *sabras* (native-born). Like the local cactus fruit they're named after, sabras have tough, thorny exteriors, but they're soft and sweet inside. Sabras come in an astonishing array, from the dentist water-skiing in her "dental floss" bikini to a yoga teacher hitchhiking home to Beersheva for the Sabbath, to a student speeding on his Yamaha to his business Arabic course at Haifa University.

Minority Communities

- ### Arab Israelis

About one Israeli in five is an Arab. Some are farmers in white *keffiye* headdress, others are merchants, teachers, members of the diplomatic corps or the Knesset (parliament). (Among the country's fastest growing minorities, they have the power to elect as many as 14 out of 120 Knesset seats. In July, 1996, the Knesset opened a special prayer room for Moslem members.) About 6,000 of them study at Israeli universities — some carry laptop computers, others, worry beads.

About 87 percent of Arab Israelis are Sunni Moslems (the rest are Christians) and many of them live according to the strictures of the Koran. While most of the country's 900,000 Arabs are loyal citizens, many also have sympathies with their brothers and sisters across Israel's borders. To avoid any conflicts of loyalty that might pose an internal security threat, Arabs are not required to serve in Israel's army.

A growing number of programs encourage Jewish-Arab joint business ventures. Because of their experience in Israel's economy and their connection to Palestinians and other Middle Eastern Arabs, Israeli Arabs are in a key position to help build economic ties between Israel and the Arab world.

The Rabin assassination gave many Israeli Arabs a new sense of belonging. Like the Jews, some cried in front of their TVs, mourning the loss of a man determined to advance peace. After the 1996 suicide bomb attacks in Tel Aviv and Jerusalem, thousands of Arab Israelis held rallies protesting the terrorism.

But despite decades of living together, most Arabs and Jews continue to live very separate lives. Though few Arab Israelis believe in *jihad* (holy war against the Jews) and less than one percent have engaged in terrorism, tensions between Israeli Jews and Arabs still surface after a terrorist attack.

- **Bedouin & Druze**

Israel's 70,000 Bedouin belong to over 30 tribes scattered throughout the Negev region in the south. Originally nomadic desert shepherds, many now live in villages and work in industry, construction, transportation and tourism. Bedouin volunteers in Israel's army are valued as trackers and scouts.

There are approximately 80,000 Druze. Many of them serve in Israel's army at their own request, and many have been decorated for bravery. A tightly-knit religious community, they broke away from Islam in the eleventh century. Today, they live mainly in the Galilee, in the Carmel mountains near Haifa, and in Syria and Lebanon. Many work as farmers or as members of the diplomatic and press corps, and they own Israel's first yacht-building firm.

Cultural Stereotypes

Guns & Tractors

Israelis are soldier-farmers living on communes.

A strikingly handsome, bronzed man plows a field with an Uzi slung over his shoulder. Nearby, a brunette in khaki shorts and sandals picks oranges. At night, they sing and dance the *hora* around a campfire. They live on a *kibbutz*, a collective farm. Almost everything — food, shelter, clothing, medical care and education — is provided by the community. *Kibbutzniks* have both the best military record and the highest war casualty rate of any group in the country. They're intensely involved in politics. About one third of Israel's cabinet ministers and four of its prime ministers — from General Moshe Dayan to Prime Minister David Ben Gurion — have been kibbutzniks.

But the truth is that, in 1996, only about 2.4 percent of Israelis live on a kibbutz; still, they produce 45 percent of the country's agriculture. Instead of milking cows or ploughing fields, more and more kibbutzniks are making medical imaging equipment or CD-ROMs. More than two-thirds of kibbutz income now comes from kibbutz-owned factories (all 400 of them). *Kibbutzim* also have become far less socialistic. No longer is all property, except for minor personal belongings, communally owned; no longer are children raised collectively in separate children's homes. Most of Israel's 269 kibbutzim (with 100 to 2,000 members each) function like independent societies within a larger capitalistic one.

Nosy & Tactless

Israelis have no respect for privacy.

Your taxi driver asks, "Are you married? No??? You're so pretty. Why not?" A hotel clerk inquires: "Do you have children?" then adds, "Why not?" You may find these remarks meddling and invasive, but many Israelis see them as reflections of warmth and friendliness, a way of treating someone like family. It's a group-oriented society; people often have difficulty understanding the Western concept of "private space."

If your Israeli host asks how much you're paying for your hotel room, it's probably because he doesn't want you to be *fryer*, someone who gets taken. If he thinks you should be paying less, he'll tell you. Before a business meeting, you might see employees standing around the water cooler, comparing paychecks. A secretary might notice your briefcase and say: "How nice. How much did you pay for it?" By Israeli standards, this is admiration, not a lack of tact. In Israeli offices, co-workers often act like a family group, meddling, squabbling and bragging. There are few physical or emotional barriers between them. They find it strange to work in offices where employees "guard their privacy" in separate cubicles.

Israelis also value close relations with neighbors. Image that you've just sneaked away from the office to relax on your apartment balcony. From a nearby window, a neighbor yells out, "Oh, so you're home early? I've got to run to the proctologist. Keep an eye on my kids, okay?" It's hard to keep a secret in Israel, but it's also hard to be lonely.

Israel is one of the world's most densely populated countries, and it's filled with people who'll bluntly point out that you're not eating enough or that you're dating a jerk. Closeness promotes cohesion, but it also means that people know the intimate details of each other's lives. It's almost impossible to remain anonymous. Maybe that's one reason why about 40 percent of the country's adults travel abroad each year — away from the pressure cooker atmosphere and from concerned family and friends.

Famous for Being Rude

In Israel, the term "customer service" is an oxymoron.

Until recently, Israel was known for its rude salespeople, inattentive clerks and Byzantine bureaucrats. This once-socialist society is undergoing a surprisingly rapid capitalistic reversal. Bank tellers and postal workers are friendly and efficient. In many restaurants, waitresses no longer dump plates on customers' tables and then shrug their shoulders. And if you complain about your overcooked steak, it's likely to be whisked away and replaced without charge.

As more Israelis travel, study and work abroad, they import exotic new ideas, like customer service. Even the Shekem — a former Army supply store where customers were treated like boot-camp recruits — is now run like a mini-version of Bloomingdales. While Israel doesn't have Japan's level of service (and probably never will), it's astoundingly better than ever. Still, if you stand back and "wait your turn," you may be ignored or overtaken in line. If you've ever waited for a bus or stood in line for a popular movie in Israel, you've undoubtedly noticed that Israelis are allergic to waiting and to lines.

You won't meet terminally perky salespeople flashing broad, "your wish is my command" smiles. Israelis perceive this behavior as disingenuous and robot-like. If a waitress asks how you are, she'll expect an honest reply. "A toothache, you have?" She might forget the other diners while she goes in search of an aspirin, then writes down the name of her cousin, the dentist. Israeli service people tend to treat customers like individuals, rather then assembly-line products.

If you haven't visited Israel since 1990, you'll be shocked. It's not provincial anymore. Israelis are among the world's top users of home computers, cellular phones and ATMs. Almost everyone uses credit cards. Groceries can be ordered by phone, and some supermarket chains keep computerized records of customer complaints — from the freshness of the meat to the sweetness of the oranges (or lack thereof). The post office has a special pick-up and express service (that actually works). Customers at Bank Leumi's 230 branches can get their own "personal banker," so that they don't have to go to separate checking and credit departments. Watch out, though. Your "personal" banker may ask why you're not married yet.

Road Warriors

Israelis drive like maniacs.

Israelis are among the world's worst drivers. If you drive too slowly, they may yell at you out the window and weave between lanes. If a traffic cop isn't in sight, why obey the rules? That white line in the middle of the road is just a suggestion. Israelis admire bending, challenging and changing rules. If a policeman stops someone, he might begin gesticulating wildly, arguing that the law is stupid.

Many Israelis tailgate because they can't bear to have anyone cut ahead of them. If the light turns green and you don't floor the gas pedal instantly, you'll be barraged with impatient honks. There are approximately twice as many road deaths in Israel, per kilometer driven, as in either the United States or the United Kingdom. The number of cars has increased 90 percent in the last decade. With 1.4 million of them on the road, there are more per kilometer than in any other country.

When former Jerusalem mayor Teddy Kollek was asked why Israelis are such terrible drivers, he said, "When you have to fight a war once every ten years, safe driving becomes the farthest thing from your mind."

6   Piety & Politics

Judaism is a 4,000-year-old civilization and
Jews are a "people" who share a common heritage
— history, language and religion. They are not a
race. While Christianity and Islam trace their ori-
gins to Judaism and are heavily influenced by it,
Judaism remains distinct from both. Jews acknowl-
edge one indivisible God of mercy, justice and
morality, a belief for which they've suffered centuries of persecution, enslavement and genocide.

Israelis practice their religion in different ways:
the level of observance ranges from the ultra-
Orthodox *yeshiva* student who looks as if he came
out of a Polish *shtetl* (village) in his black coat, fur
hat, beard and sidecurls; to the modern Orthodox
doctor in a *kipa* (small knit skull cap); to the non-
Orthodox physicist who eats (unkosher) cheesebur-
gers and drives on the Sabbath. Over two-thirds of
Israelis are non-Orthodox or secular, and they
cover a broad range — from vehemently anti-reli-
gious to those who observe some Jewish traditions.
About 56 percent attend High Holiday services for
Rosh Hashanah and Yom Kippur and 71 percent
fast on Yom Kippur (see Customs, Chapter 20).
Since about 1990, the number of non-Orthodox

(Reform and Conservative) rabbis and gender-equal synagogues has been growing.

The Power of Orthodoxy

Though only about 16 percent of the country's Jews are Orthodox, their rabbis hold a monopoly on much of Israel's religious life. (Because of their high birthrate, ultra-Orthodox Jews and Arab Moslems are the fastest growing members of society.)

Governments are formed with the narrowest of margins. Both the left-leaning Labor and the right-leaning Likud parties often look for allies among the dozen or so smaller political groups (ranging from Russian immigrants to the Islamic movement). Politicians from Orthodox parties have been awarded powerful ministries — including Education, Interior, Religion, Labor and Welfare — and Orthodox Jews have received massive government subsidies for their synagogues and *yeshivot* (religious academies).

Orthodox rabbis are the only ones allowed to perform marriages (which means that thousands of couples must go abroad for civil ceremonies) and religious conversions. Orthodox women and full-time ultra-Orthodox religious students are exempt from the military. *Kashrut* (religious dietary observance) is enforced in Israel's army (the Israeli Defense Forces or IDF) and in many public places. Some Orthodox Jews want the government to authorize the closure of certain roads, as well as all restaurants, movie theatres and other entertainments on the Sabbath — the official "day of rest" during which they refrain from work of any kind, including writing letters or driving a car.

Officially, Israel is a secular state. It has no formal constitution, in part because many Orthodox and ultra-Orthodox Israelis want one based on traditional Judaic laws, while most other Israelis don't. Lacking an official definition of religious parameters, Orthodox rabbis and politicians have been using their influence to pass what some see as coersive laws. Many liberal Israelis are waging legal wars to lessen the Orthodoxy's clout. Meanwhile, Orthodox politicians won an unprecedented 23 seats in the 1996 election, up from 16 in the previous Knesset.

Three Israelis = Four Parties

Politics is Israel's lifeblood. A well-known saying goes: If there are three Israelis in a room, there will be at least four political parties. David Ben-Gurion once told Dwight Eisenhower, "You're president of 200 million people, but I'm prime minister of two million prime ministers." Israelis rarely agree on any political subject. For riveting theatrical drama and mudslinging, watch Knesset (parliament) debates — they range from fiery to raucous to hilarious. (Visitors are welcome, and some debates are televised.)

The only Western-style democracy in the Middle East, Israel has a free press and judiciary and civil rights. The 120 Knesset members are elected by citizens over the age of eighteen. In 1996, Israelis started electing their prime minister by direct ballot. American-style public relations consultants are training politicians (like Prime Minister Benjamin Netanyahu) to be more telegenic and to speak in "sound bites." Immigrants who've fled totalitarian states (like the former Soviet Union or Iran) get quickly swept up into Israel's hyperactive, argumentative democracy. Truck drivers, dental hygienists — everyone has strong political opinions. If you have high blood pressure, don't argue politics with an Israeli. And don't even begin unless you have hours to spare.

7

The Army

Living on the Edge

Israelis always have lived with air raid sirens and bomb shelters. Whenever Hizbollah terrorists in south Lebanon launch Katyusha rockets into Israel's Galilee, parents frantically search for their children. During the Gulf War, when thirty-nine of Saddam Hussein's Scud missiles rained down on Tel Aviv, Israelis ran to the protection of sealed rooms, hoping that their gas masks would protect them from nerve gas made of German chemicals — an eerie reminder of the Nazi gas chambers. Life on the edge has created in Israelis a directness and an astonishing patriotic depth. Many citizens have fought in three or four different wars during the last fifty years — the War of Independence (1947-48), the Suez Campaign (1956), the Six Day War (1967), the War of Attrition (1968-70), the Yom Kippur War (1973) and the Lebanon War (1982), as well as numerous random terror attacks. They accept the constant tension by adopting an attitude of *ein brera* — "no other choice" — an almost fatalistic acceptance of living in a country that, despite the peace agreements of the 1990s, is always one radio report away from tragedy.

Young Israelis are drafted willingly into the Israel Defense Forces (IDF) and many volunteer for combat units. Israel demands more service in the military than any other country in the world. It's also the only country that drafts women. At 18, men are drafted for at least three years, unmarried non-Orthodox women for 20 months. Men spend much of their lives in and out of uniform. A 20-year-old soldier commands a unit that patrols the border with Lebanon 'round the clock. Daily, he faces new pressures, including how to keep cool under fire. Living with frequent emergencies and tragedies, Israelis get tough. Many of the traits found in Israeli business people were forged in the IDF — including a lack of formality and the ability to improvise and react well during crises.

Melting Pot & Matchmaker

Serving in the IDF is one of the most truly Israeli experiences. Here, Israelis with different ethnic and economic backgrounds — from the yuppie sabra to the Ukrainian-born violinist — live and die together. Most serve between the formative ages of 18 and 21. A *sabra* with a knitted *kipa* yells out, saving his Iraqi-Israeli jeep mate from driving onto a land mind. An Ethiopian-Israel F16 pilot who grew up in a remote village gossips with his Italian-Israeli co-pilot. They speak their new common language, Hebrew, Israeli-style: tersely and bluntly. Because many remain with the same group of soldiers throughout their active military and reserve years, strong friendships are forged, and some carry over from the battlefield into the boardroom.

The IDF is also a powerful matchmaker. A Moroccan-Israeli lieutenant teaches French to a blonde American-Israel private; that night, they conjugate verbs while she keeps him company on guard duty. The IDF is very informal. The age difference between a soldier and commanding officer is often no more than a year. Officers and soldiers address each other by first names, wear the same unimpressive uniforms, eat the same foods and rarely use military titles.

A Peoples' Army

Because Israel's population is so small, the IDF is primarily an army of civilians who temporarily put on uniforms. Soldiers mingle freely with the populace — from pilots dancing samba at a Tel Aviv disco to the uniformed reserve officer, still carrying his sub-machine gun, rushing into a software meeting. Until age 49, most men spend about 30 to 40 days a year in active reserve service. A Tel Aviv University professor's naval reserve commanding officer might be his engineering student. A bank president may report to his car mechanic.

Though Israelis willingly serve in the IDF, most can't stand war anymore. Many of the doves leading the peace movement today are former high-ranking military officers. Over a hundred thousand Israelis were rallying for peace when a religious fundamentalist tried to stop it by assassinating Yitzhak Rabin. The last words of this soldier-turned-peacemaker were, "The nation of Israel wants peace, supports peace...."

Pilots = CEOs

The spin-off from Israeli military and defense related industries into the civilian field is very important to Israeli businesses. Some of Israel's finest civilian engineers came from the Israeli Army's technical units. Many small companies have former Israeli officers, especially Air Force pilots, as their CEOs.

8 Government & Business

No Dinosaurs

Despite impressive economic growth under the Labor government — an impressive $90 billion GNP — the new Likud government says it will make economic reform a top priority. Soon after his May 29th 1996 election victory, Prime Minister Netanyahu (an MBA from Massachusetts Institute of Technology's Sloan School of Management) unveiled sweeping proposals to lower taxes, lift regulatory barriers and privatize the heavily state-run economy.

Netanyahu says Israel's potential for having one of the world's most productive economies is shackled by centralized planning and a rigid bureaucracy; he wants his government to dismantle those barriers. With the help of Finance Minister Dan Meridor, he will likely speed up privatization by allowing the public to buy shares in such state-run companies as Telecom, the airline El Al and major banks. Israel, he said recently, has been saddled with "twin curses" — an extremely large defense industry and a socialist economy — but that those obstacles have become "twin blessings." Israel's defense industry has created an enormous pool of highly educated workers, and socialism never burdened Israel with the outmoded industries that now dragging down Europe and, to a lesser extent, the United States. "As a result," he said, "there are no dinosaurs walking around."

Wooing High Tech Investors

Israel is second after the U.S. in the amount of venture capital relative to the size of the economy, according to a recent study. Multinationals pouring in funds include Nestle, Intel, Volkswagen and Motorola. In the U.S., only about two-thirds of venture capital goes into technology; in Israel, it's 100 percent. Between 1991 and 1994, the amount of venture capital swelled by a factor of 10 — to US$500 million. Two-thirds of it comes from abroad. In 1995, overseas investors poured in US$2.3 billion into promising Israeli start-ups, joint ventures, mergers and acquisitions. International investment banking houses with offices in Israel include Lehman Bros. Salomon, Smith Barney, Goldman Sachs and Merrill Lynch, as well as key financiers of California's Silicon Valley.

Netanyahu hopes to lure even more investment from top Wall Street money houses. Soon after his election, he made a rousing luncheon speech at the New York Stock Exchange to about 150 of America's most powerful executives and corporate financiers. Within a decade, he said, "we could have an economy of a quarter trillion dollars. An economy with the most powerful resource of all: a gifted people with a technological base, able to compete in the world marketplace of tomorrow."

During the first five months of 1996, almost a third of the 36 new foreign issues on NASDAQ were Israeli companies. (Israel is second only to Canada for the number of its companies publicly traded on NASDAQ). And Netanyahu has promised that "many more" Israeli stocks will be traded on the New York Stock Exchange during his administration than the current three. There are presently over eighty Israeli companies on the three New York stock exchanges.

Netanyahu's government is continuing what the previous Labor administration began: developing roads, pipelines, a Tel Aviv regional commuter rail, and spending about $830 million to expand Ben Gurion Airport. Tourism and business travel are expanding rapidly: In 1995, seven million travelers boarded over 30,000 international flights to or from Israel, and the annual figure is expected to reach 16 million within the next two decades.

Government Encourages Entrepreneurs

Government cooperation is bound up in almost every start-up operation. In 1995, for example, the chief scientist's office of the Ministry of Industry and Trade gave $346 million in grants to 1,213 civilian Research & Development projects. After receiving these, many Israeli firms then get investments from international venture capitalists.

A number of government-assisted international companies are opening facilities in Israel:

- The single largest European investment in Israel is a $350 million partnership between Volkswagen and Dead Sea Works to manufacture magnesium parts (the lightweight metal is increasingly popular with automakers). The Israeli government subsidized 38 percent of the project's total cost — about US$133 million.

- The cornerstone had been laid for the new Intel factory in Kiryat Gat that will produce flash memory for mobile telephones and computers.

The total investment will be US$1.6 billion, 38 percent of which will be funded by an Israeli Government grant. Peak production capacity is expected to be $1 billion per year.

- Rockwell Semiconductor Systems and Analog Devices (one of the largest semiconductor companies in the U.S.) are establishing Israeli research and development centers.

- Johnson & Johnson will open in Israel in 1997.

- Smith Barney, one of Wall Street's leading investment banks, is opening an Israeli office.

- Vishay Intertechnology, manufacturer of a range of electronic resistors and sensors, opened its fourth plant, a US$175 million factory in Migdal Ha'emek, to produce multilayer ceramic capacitors for electronic equipment.

- The Italian insurance company, Generali, has recently invested US$400 million in return for 40 percent of Israel's largest insurance company.

9 The New Business Climate

Israel is no longer an emerging market: it has emerged. Israel is among the twenty richest countries in the world and living standards are high. The Bank of Israel says $2.1 billion was pumped into the economy in 1995 by overseas investors, which is over twice the 1994 level. Israel's white-hot economic growth should hit 6 percent in 1996. Foreign investors are building factories, setting up R&D facilities, buying up Israeli companies and forming strategic alliances. "Corporations are beginning to understand that the Israeli economy provides all sorts of opportunities for them, not just in terms of marketing, but also in terms of investment," says Martin Indyk, the U.S. Ambassador to Israel. "Word is getting out that Israel is a potential 'Asian tiger' in the Middle East."

From Socialism to Free Enterprise

In 1985, Israel had an inefficient socialist economy crippled by South American-style inflation. Then the government restructured the cumbersome state-controlled system. Its sweeping pro-growth reforms included trade liberalization, privatization of government monopolies, the removal of unnecessary currency controls and the elimination of much red tape. The budget deficit was curbed, ending its galloping 1985 inflation rate of 450 percent. By 1995, inflation had been reduced to a manageable 8 percent.

In 1985, the GDP was $22 billion; ten years later, it had quadrupled. In 1960, almost 70 percent of Israel's exports were agricultural products; today, these constitute only 2 percent, while high-tech products (microprocessors, CD-ROMs, medical diagnostic equipment and biotech/telecom/software protection systems) make up 60 percent. Israel is the third-largest exporting nation in the world on a per-capita basis.

Israel is the only country that has Free Trade Agreements with Europe (the E.U. and E.F.T.A.), the United States and Canada, and it spends a higher percentage of its GDP on research and development than any other nation. With its small economy and limited domestic market, Israel must expand exports to boost growth.

Brain Power

Israel has few natural resources but an abundance of intellectual capital. As previously mentioned, the influx of highly educated Jews from the former Soviet Union has boosted Israel's brain power. (In certain high tech industries, about 30 percent of the engineers are recent Russian immigrants.) Per capita, Israel has the world's highest number of engineers and scientists; the U.S. has 70 per 10,000 people, while Israel has 135 per 10,000. And three times more of them are engaged in research and development per capita than anywhere else. According to former Prime Minister Shimon Peres, in 1996, "Israel will make more out of her brains than the Saudis will make out of their oil wells." (Israel's annual per capita GNP is about $16,000, compared with the Saudi's $6,000). Twenty-six percent of Israeli professionals work in technical fields (compared with 18 percent in the U.S.), and Israel ranks ahead of Japan, Britain, Sweden and The Netherlands in the percentage of people seeking higher education.

Israelis are world leaders in biomedical and agri-tech research. Israeli scientists have produced sophisticated magnetic resonance image machines, ultra fast x-ray imaging cameras, and improved breast cancer and prenatal diagnosis. Researchers have discovered new drugs or treatments for cancers (including leukemia, ovarian cancer, malignant melanoma), multiple sclerosis, herpes, hepatitis B, arthritis, lupus and osteoporosis, developed anti-tumor vaccines, improved bone-marrow transplants and new treatments for infertility and heart attack victims. Israeli scientists have developed items ranging from more nutritious potatoes and strains of wheat with twice the protein of other varieties to innovative solar energy technologies and fire-resistant plastics.

The High Tech Promised Land

Israel is as close to the technological cutting edge as the U.S, or any country in Europe. Your automobile was probably designed, in part, on a software system created by an Israeli company, Cimatron. When you read a magazine (such as *Time, Sports Illustrated* or *National Geographic*), there's a good chance that the color printing used a system developed by Israel's Scitex. The Intel 486 chip on your personal computer was designed (and likely manufactured) in Israel. The Intel 8088 microprocessor — the "brains" of the original IBC PC that helped

spark a worldwide personal computer revolution —
was born here, too. In 1998, Intel will open its third
facility in Israel, a $1.6 billion flash memory chip
plant. This represents the largest foreign investment
ever made in Israel. (Israel encourages foreign capital investments and start-ups with cash grants and
excellent tax breaks.) In 1996, Israel's first communications satellite, Amos, was launched in French Guy-
ana. (It's expected to provide improved services for
cable TV, cellular phones and on-line data links.)
About 3,000 new tech companies have been formed
here since 1990.

Peace = Investment Opportunities

In 1993, there was almost no foreign investment
in Israel, because many companies were afraid of
being blacklisted by Arab states. But since then, the
picture has changed radically. Due in great measure
to the signing of the Oslo Peace Accords, 50+ countries have made ties with Israel. El Al, the national
airline (which had lost business for decades
because many countries were too intimidated by
the Arab boycott to offer landing rights) has more
than doubled its number of destinations.

Encouraged by the peace process, Israel has
made a dramatic shift from using its expertise for
military fields to applying it to innovative civilian
commerce. In 1967, the defense budget ate up a
whopping 30 percent of the GDP; today, it accounts
for less than 10 percent. Previously, Europe and the
U.S. had been Israel's biggest markets. But with the
erosion of the Arab boycott, 45 percent of Israeli
exports now go to such previously closed markets
as China, South Korea, Vietnam, Indonesia and
India.

An Israeli company is installing the air traffic
control system in Hong Kong's new airport. Other

Israeli companies are installing new phone systems in Eastern Europe and parts of the former Soviet Union. And Israeli exports in telecom, computerized medical electronics, agri tech and educational software are skyrocketing.

Trade with Asia has grown over 85 percent since 1990. Japan opened a trade office in 1995 and is already Israel's second largest export market. As a Japanese official explained, "Israelis are great at innovation and have a Japanese sense of teamwork and loyalty to the company."

Briefcases, Not Guns

Of the $20 billion that will be earned in export markets in 1996, only 1/50th will derive from exports to the Arab world. But this meager percentage is destined to change in the future as Israelis and Arabs — separated by almost fifty years of conflict — plan joint ventures and import-export arrangements worth billions of U.S. dollars. Businesspeople from the Gulf states, Saudi Arabia, Jordan and Egypt are arriving in Israel with briefcases instead of guns. Israel and Jordan are currently planning over US$25 billion worth of projects, from joint water conservation to international roads, railways and canals.

In July 1996, Israel and Egypt co-signed a deal to build the Middle East Oil Refinery, a US$1 billion investment, in Alexandria. It's expected to yield up to 100,000 barrels a day.

Arabs + Israelis = Tourism

A joint Israeli-Jordanian Red Sea international airport, Shalom-Salaam, will serve the adjacent port cities of Eilat and Aqaba and open up the Red Sea Riviera. Royal Jordanian Airlines and El Al are flying regularly between Israel and Jordan. Jordanian and Israeli motorists can now drive across the border. Tourism in both Jordan and Israel is now a major source of revenue. International tourists spent $2.5 billion in Israel in 1995, and the figure is expected to triple over the next ten years. "I think that tourism may have a greater effect upon the Middle East than the wars," says former Prime Minister Shimon Peres. "If you ask me what will bring more security -- a hotel or a military position, I'd say a hotel."

10 The Work Environment

Small Town Atmosphere

Many Israeli offices resemble small towns. People talk loudly, shmooze and gossip, and the line between their professional and private lives is often thin (if not invisible). "I guess I seemed stand-offish and distant because I used to drink coffee at my desk," says an English computer programmer who was based in Haifa for three years. "After a few weeks, I joined them (my Israeli co-workers) during coffee breaks. Then I really saw their warmth. When my wife got sick, everyone offered advice about doctors and my boss ordered me to leave work early. In Israel, family comes first. When I mentioned I was buying an apartment, two co-workers volunteered to be guarantors on my mortgage. I hadn't even asked them. In England, I wouldn't have dared ask *my best friend* to co-sign."

Some Israelis who have worked abroad (in non-Mediterranean and non-Latin countries) find office atmospheres there unfriendly or lonely. "After only two weeks in my Tel Aviv office, I knew more about my co-workers than I did after two years in America," says an Israeli computer software designer who works for a Seattle company.

He says his American co-workers "rarely show their true emotions. They smile a lot and ask, 'How are you?' but they don't really care. People work together, yet never visit each other's homes."

The Israeli work environment tends to promote group cooperation, rather than competition. An Israeli lawyer who worked in a Washington D.C. law firm describes her American co-workers as "coldly competitive," adding, "In America, I kept hearing words, like 'self-esteem' and 'self-reliant.' I rarely hear those words in Hebrew. Our (Tel Aviv) office is a collective 'we.' We're a team. We share both the blame and the glory."

"Why Do It Your Way?"

Usually, Israelis are more interested in goals than roles, and the lack of difference in status between bosses, managers and secretaries stuns some outsiders. Instead of hierarchical leadership, many prefer leadership by "natural authority." In some offices, it seems as though *everyone's* in charge. You might overhear a secretary lose her temper with her boss and loudly blurt out, "Yossi, what are you talking about? Are you crazy?" Such behavior might strike outsiders as insubordinate, but to Israelis, it's honest and direct.

Many Israelis love to challenge authority. "When I tell my Israeli engineers to do something, they start arguing. 'Why do it this way? Why not that way?' At first, their attitude drove me crazy," says an American CEO of a Massachusetts telecommunications company with a Tel Aviv subsidiary. "But now, I love having these Israelis who improvise and innovate. I'm smiling all the way to the bank."

Risk Takers

In many countries, employees are expected to work within a system. But in Israel, workers test and bend rules. You might see a bank official sitting in a cloud of cigarette smoke, ignoring both the "No Smoking" sign above her and the law that bans smoking in public places. In the workplace, if you go by the rules, you might be seen as afraid, rigid, or lacking initiative. Finding short cuts and taking risks are considered virtues. "If you tell an American the shortest distance between two dots is a straight line, he'll take it for granted," says the Massachusetts CEO. "An Israeli will try to find an even shorter way. If you're looking for shortcuts to save on costs and make money, he'll find them."

Creative Problem Solving

When France stopped selling Mirage fighter planes to Israel after the Six Day War in 1967, Israel started its own defense industry. Many Israelis prize a particular story of a soldier stationed in the Sinai during the 1973 war. His tank was misfiring, but he didn't have tools, so he used the hair pin holding his *kipa* (skullcap) to fix it. Life in Israel means learning to expect the unexpected. "In America, if you don't have an antenna to operate your communications equipment, you wait until headquarters sends it. An Israeli will find a wire and stretch it between two trees," said one former IDF colonel. "When the technical manual says you need parts A, B, and C and part C is missing, Israelis don't wait for it; they improvise. Because so many countries obeyed the Arab boycott, for decades we've gone without a lot of things and had to improvise with what we had."

When citrus exports were facing stiff competition from Greece, Italy and Spain, Israeli growers began exporting flowers to Europe in winter. They'd discovered that flowers took up less space than orange groves and could be raised in hot houses. Today, flowers outnumber citrus exports (which dropped from 11 percent in 1970 to 0.7 percent in 1994). For almost fifty years, Israeli volunteers with expertise in innovative, low-cost agri-tech have been working in many developing nations in Africa, Latin America and Asia/Pacific, as well as training students in Israel. (Israel has the highest producing cows and the highest yield of wheat per acre in the world, and most of the world's cucumbers come from a new Israeli hybrid.) Recently, insects threatened to destroy much of Fiji's ginger crop, and export customers refused to buy ginger that had been sprayed by pesticides. The Fijians called in an Israeli agronomy expert, who covered the fields with sheets of a new Israeli plastic that raised the ground temperature and killed the insects.

Balagan = Organized Chaos

"Israelis have the right mix of creativity and discipline," says the co-founder of a leading Israeli biotech firm. "Development is particularly cost-effective here in the land of well-organized *balagan* (disorder or mess)." America, he explains, "is the land of standardization. In the U.S., when I need to deal with drug approvals, I get a stomach ache. If the instructions say the margins on the application page must be one-third of an inch and mine is one-quarter, the Americans will return the whole application and make me start the whole process over. Israelis are less finicky."

A few years ago, a Ministry of Foreign Affairs official was awaiting foreign dignitaries, who were coming to inspect a prototype of the Lavie airplane at Israel Aviation Industries. "Workers were in blue jeans and sandals and stained shirts. It was a *bala-gan*, with hammers, pliers and screws all over the place," he recalls. "I told the foreman that if he was trying to sell planes, he should make the workplace orderly, get the workers to look professional. He answered 'Why? If everything is clean and neat, that means we're putting all our energy into looking good, instead of working. Who cares what the place looks like if our planes fly great.' "For Israelis — who've produced the world-famous Kfir fighters and remote pilotless planes — appearances are a lot less important than results.

A New Breed of Entrepreneurs

A rapidly growing faction of internationally-minded Israelis are filling language classes in business Arabic, Japanese or Chinese. Many have studied and worked abroad and learned marketing, advertising and public relations, which are new fields in Israel. Many speak the international language of high tech. Visitors are surprised to see how much Israeli high-tech industrial parks resemble their counterparts in Silicon Valley, both externally and internally.

11 Women in Business

Traditional Roles

Israeli women are "strong," "emancipated" and "sexually liberated." Like all stereotypes, this one is partially true. Pioneer women drained swamps, built roads and sang songs of equality. Brave female soldiers fought on the front lines during Israel's War of Independence. Today, women still drive tractors and hold key positions in kibbutz factories — but they've always outnumbered men in kibbutz laundries, kitchens and kindergartens. Women corporals train male privates to fire guns and drive tanks, but it wasn't until 1996 that the Air Force admitted women into pilot training courses. An orthodox woman can be divorced by her husband, but she cannot divorce him.

Golda Meir was one of the world's only female prime ministers (the late Prime Minister David Ben-Gurion dubbed her "the only man in my government"), but not many women politicians have followed in her footsteps. Prior to the 1996 election, women held 12 out of 120 Knesset seats; currently, they hold nine.

The Middle East, as a whole, has the world's lowest rate of female employment (9 percent); in contrast, 52 percent of Israeli women work. However, since husbands are called to military reserve duty each year, many working mothers spend more time with their children than they do on career fast tracks. Until there's genuine peace in the Middle East, true gender equality will be difficult. "When a nation is at war, all other societal issues are secondary," says one Israeli feminist. "Sexual equality is secondary to survival. Israeli women are second to the male 'warrior-soldier.' "

Trends

In 1961, there were virtually no Israeli women in top and middle management positions. Today, over 24 percent of these positions are held by women. In 1996, the Knesset passed a law giving Israeli women the same salaries and benefits as their male counterparts. And there's been a dramatic upswing in the number of women directors at government-owned companies (especially since the Israel Supreme Court upheld a 1992 law requiring affirmative action). But women are still rare in Israeli boardrooms in the private sector.

One of the first Israeli women to make a significant mark on the business world was Lea Gottleib. Her company, Gottex, is the world's top producer of designer bathing suits (with exports to over 90 countries and a 60 percent share of the U.S. designer swimwear market). Two Israeli women single-handedly put Israel on the international art auction map when they opened a Sotheby's in Tel Aviv. A top Israeli high-tech consulting firm was started by two Israeli women with Harvard MBAs. In June 1995, when Galia Maor was appointed head of Bank Leumi (Israeli's second largest bank), the local press focused on her economic acumen, not her gender. That same year, Aliza Shenhar, the first woman to head an Israeli (Haifa) university, became Israel's new Ambassador to Russia. And in 1996, Labor Minister Ora Namir was appointed Ambassador to China.

Chromosomes & Family Issues

"I encounter many more cross-cultural issues being an American in Israel than as a woman in Israel," says a software marketing executive who worked with Israeli high tech companies for three years. "Savvy Israeli businessmen will appreciate your skills, whether you have a different chromosome or not. If you're outspoken and strong, they take you seriously. If you don't play "the weak woman," you'll be treated as an equal. As an American businesswoman, I was trained to be nice and accommodating. Working in Israel taught me to get right to the point and say what I mean. I'm now using those skills in my Boston office."

The Israeli workplace tends to respect family issues. An Israeli high-tech executive who works in Silicon Valley put it like this. "In Palo Alto [California], I hire baby-sitters whenever my kids are sick. I'm afraid to take time off. In Israel, whenever anyone had a family emergency, my (Israeli) boss was understanding and flexible. I miss my Tel Aviv office. It was such an extended family that you often saw your children playing there after school."

Flirting

An English computer programmer who has lived in Israel for 18 years says, "I find a lot of pluses being a businesswoman in Israel. It's certainly more fun than in England and America. I've used harmless flirting to butter up my macho Israeli boss — I've gotten him to sign contracts my male colleagues couldn't. Many Israeli men enjoy trying to get a woman's adrenaline going. Part of it's ego, most of it's a game." Now, she works for a San Francisco branch of the same company, where the atmosphere is "asexual." She adds, "If I tried to use my womanly charms here, men wouldn't take notice for fear of law suits."

In an Israeli meeting, a businessman might give a female associate a nickname like *meydeleh* (Yiddish for "little girl"). To him, it's a sign of affection, not condescension. During the meeting, he might touch her hand, noting in a velvety voice, "Your eyes are so beautiful." To him, it's a compliment, not a sexual suggestion. When he learns that she's the marketing director, he might ask, incredulously, "You're just a baby. How old are you?" To him, it's praise, not prying. And at the meeting's end, he just might embrace his associate with a good-bye bear hug.

If rampant flirting makes you feel uncomfortable, ignore it. Rarely will an Israeli man make a sexual move if a woman isn't responding. Let's say he misinterprets your friendly smile as an invitation. He might look deep into your eyes, squeeze your hand and gush, "Does your boyfriend appreciate that gorgeous smile?" Pull your hand back and answer firmly, "Yes, and I'm very faithful." An unattached American-Israeli radio reporter estimated that men asked her if she was married at least four times a day. Finally, she bought herself a ring, and whenever a man asked, she held up her ring finger. The questions stopped.

But for all the admiration and attention, it's noteworthy that women in Israel can walk alone safely, even at night (but keep to well-lit areas). The crime rate is very low; Seattle, Washington has seven times more murders than Jerusalem.

 12 **Making Connections**

Doing business is usually easier with the help of friends or contacts. Israel is so small that when two Israelis meet for the first time, they often discover within minutes that they have friends in common. For this reason, it's not difficult to find out whom you need to know. The key Israeli players in your field probably know each other.

Easy Access

Contacting high level Israeli officials is usually much easier than getting in touch with their European or American counterparts. Israelis are amazingly accessible. Many mayors and Knesset members list their home telephone numbers in public directories. Don't be afraid to call the CEO of a company, even before you arrive in the country. If you don't have a name to drop, just say, "It was suggested I ring you." It's stunning how open the Israeli business community is to outsiders. Once you know at least one Israel in the right field, it's usually easy to "network."

But don't get too excited if the managing director of a large Israeli firm invites you to a long, friendly lunch. And don't think that you "have it made" when the chairman of a large Israeli bank says, "Call me at home this weekend with any questions." Though you may have gotten along wonderfully, it's not "a done deal" until the deal is done.

Favors: A Constant Exchange

Israelis rarely hesitate to ask friends or business contacts, "Asseh li tova?" ("Do me a favor?"). It's a way people build relationships, expand their contacts and, most importantly, get people to owe them. When someone owes you a favor, it's often more advantageous than if he or she owes you money.

Don't be shy about asking an Israeli for help when you need it. Ask Tali to set up a meeting with her friend Noam, the inventor of XYZ medical imaging devices. If the deal works out, you'll both owe her a favor for successful matchmaking.

An American and three other high-level executives needed emergency seats on El Al in the middle of the night. The American dealt with various ticket agents, and it turned into a mess. When he returned to Israel, he described his ordeal to his acquaintance, Uri, a mid-level official at El Al. "Why didn't you phone me at home?" asked Uri, obviously upset. "No matter it was 4 A.M., I would have arranged everything for you." Uri doesn't earn a large salary, but he would have demonstrated his power by helping the American executives. Word travels fast in Israel. Had people heard about "the favor," Uri's image as a "guy who can get things done" would have been enhanced.

Protektzia or "Vitamin P"

Knowing people who can open the right doors — that's *protektzia*, a.k.a. "Vitamin P." Protektzia is knowing the person who can put you at the head of line, it's the phone call to the person who can cut through red tape. It's hard to live without protektzia in Israel. To illustrate its power (and with typical cynical humor), Israelis invented a joke about Nazi war criminal Adolph Eichmann's trial in Jerusalem in 1961. When Eichmann was found guilty of genocide, the judge gave him a choice of punishments — "Either die by hanging or spend the rest of your days living in Israel without protektzia." Eichmann chose hanging.

Protektzia means that instead of waiting a week to get a loan approval, your bank contact gets it for you within an hour. A story goes that some years ago, a mother couldn't enroll her daughter into an elementary school class because it was full. The limit was 40 students. After she called a high-level friend at the Ministry of Education, he changed the maximum national class size to 41. A British-Israeli landed a job as a producer at Israel Television, despite the fact that she had no previous television experience. But she had protektzia — her neighbor, a news director.

Times are changing, however, and protektzia is less likely to help overcome the odds. Today, Israel has more institutional checks and balances. Official tenders and contracts are determined by quality and price. If you're nominated to be an Israeli economic consul, you must appear before a government committee, which will make sure that you're qualified (and that you're not the economic minister's best friend).

 Strategies for Success

Prepare Before You Land

Contact a knowledgeable Israeli economic attaché in a local embassy or consulate. Read about Israeli business culture, history and politics. There are some useful Israeli magazines, newspapers and newsletters in English — such as the Jerusalem Report, the Jerusalem Post and Link Magazine — and many helpful Internet Web sites (see Chapter 27).

Make Face-to-Face Contact

When you're in Israel, it's best not to do business by telephone. Personal connections can make all the difference. Face-to-face, getting-to-know-you meetings are to your advantage. Keep in mind that distances are amazingly short. You can drive from Tel Aviv to Jerusalem in less than an hour and from Jerusalem to Haifa in just over 90 minutes. It's worth fighting the traffic.

Be Flexible — and Honest

Israelis rarely plan far in advance. If you say,

"Let's have lunch two weeks from today," an Israeli might look at you strangely and respond, "Why not right now?" Be spontaneous and join him.

Don't say, "Let's meet again soon. I'll call you," unless you mean it. Israelis get offended by unkept promises. You don't want to be perceived as unreliable, or as a superficial person who "talks a good game" but never follows through. Israelis working in the same field usually know each other, and word travels fast.

Know That "No" May Mean Maybe

He said "No"? Call him again and try another approach. Consider "no" to be a challenge. You can push, or use your contacts to push for you. Israelis admire initiative and persistence. They tend to think that virtually anything is do-able and that even hard-and-fast rules are negotiable. If you're fairly sure that the no you received really does mean no, try speaking to the top person. From an Israeli point of view, if you're not willing to fight for what you want, you're not really motivated.

Learn to "Nudge" (Yiddish for "make a nuisance of yourself")

In your country, it may be impolite to phone the day after a meeting for an answer. In Israel, if someone doesn't respond as quickly as you'd like, call and ask, "So, what's happening?" Don't be afraid of alienating him or of losing the deal. It's hard to "nudge" too much. The Israeli you're pestering will probably admire your persistence. You might even develop a friendship.

If Nudging Doesn't Work, Try Guilt

Israelis generally respond to guilt. Try these examples from Guilt & Manipulation 101:

- "For this I flew fifteen hours to Israel?"
- "After what I did for you yesterday, is this how you thank me?"
- "If, God forbid, I don't get this signed by tonight, I'll miss my daughter's wedding."
- "Your employees must be incredibly busy. That's probably why no one can get me the report before my deadline."
- "Too bad you don't have an extra copy of the current Statistical Abstract. If I only had it, we could wrap this deal up quickly."

Say What You Mean

Be straightforward. If Israelis think you're sincere and not just out to make a quick dollar, you'll gain their trust and loyalty. If you're tactful and say, "This proposal sounds interesting," you might be misunderstood. Speak Israeli-style. Say bluntly, "This proposal won't work. Here's why."

Be Decisive

Some cultures tolerate or encourage uncertainty and ambiguity, but Israelis get uncomfortable if there isn't a clear resolution. Make a decision and stick with it. A well-known Israeli joke pokes fun at former Prime Minister Levi Eshkol's well-known indecisiveness. When a waiter asked Eshkol whether he'd like coffee or tea, Eshkol hesitated, and then finally stammered, "Make it *chetzi-chetzi* (half and half)."

Hire a Local Consultant, Rep or Advisor

It's often useful to have an Israeli who can guide you, read between the lines and explain what's *really* going on. When an Israeli engineer who runs a Belgian high tech company realized he didn't have up-to-date connections, he hired a local Israeli rep. Though Israeli himself, the engineer had been working abroad for eight years and was, he explained, "out of the loop. That's why I needed an Israeli who knew the right people and the latest short cuts."

It helps to have someone who understands the local games and can keep the pressure on *after* you leave. Choose an advisor, consultant or rep who understands your country's business culture and does the same type of business, whether it's real estate or bio tech. If you're selling a product in Israel, it's important to hire someone who knows how to sell it the Israeli way (which is often different from the slick, American way). Draw up a simple, short, unambiguous legal agreement. Set clear expectations about financial terms, payments, delivery schedules, inspection details and penalties. Know that even with such legal agreements, you may have to re-negotiate as the situation changes. Make certain that the Israelis you hire can communicate clearly, work the system, pressure the right people and speed the waiting time for approvals, grants or loans.

Time

Mediterranean versus Manic Modern

Time in Israel can be a confusing mix of "laid back" and ultra efficient.

A revealing joke in both Israel and Egypt goes like this :

Question: What's the difference between *mahar/bukrah* (tomorrow) and *manana*?

Answer: They're the same, only *mahar/bukrah* is less urgent.

"Your telephone will be installed tomorrow." In Israel in the 70s, "tomorrow" meant waiting for years. In the 80s, tomorrow meant months. In the 90s, tomorrow means that your phone will be connected within twenty-four hours. Doing business used to involve spending hours in long lines at different ministries, endless red tape and surly clerks. Permits were needed for almost everything — from having bank accounts in dollars to running an import-export business. There's still plenty of bureaucracy, but since the mid 80s, the Israeli government has been streamlined and greatly deregulated.

While everyday life is more efficient, Israelis still maintain a Mediterranean *joie de vivre*, which means that their attitude about time can be flexible.

If a business lunch conversation is getting juicy, why rush off to the next appointment? If an Israeli is meeting another Israeli, it's not considered rude to be at least twenty minutes late (though the one who's running behind might call on his cell phone with an excuse). But if an Israeli is meeting an international visitor or an Israeli with a German-Jewish background (a *yekke*), he's usually savvy enough to arrive on time.

Deadlines

Many Israelis don't like being controlled by watches (like they were in the army) or planning too far in advance. In Hebrew, you don't often hear expressions like "lost time," "saving time" or "Let's meet in a few months." An employee doesn't consider it "wasting time" to counsel an office mate about marital problems for an hour. His work will get finished, and hopefully on time. The Israeli tendency to do things at the last minute often means improvisation and some ad hoc (and often better) solutions.

If you ask an Israeli employee if he's finished writing a report, he might answer optimistically, "*Yihiyeh b'seder*" (which, loosely translated, means "Not to worry, everything will be fine.") That expression means that he probably hasn't started writing yet. It's wise to double check that the deadlines an Israeli sets are realistic and to keep tabs on the status of the work as the deadline approaches.

"Israelis tend to have a macho bravado, and reassure themselves that things will be fine even when they won't," says Israeli therapist and cross-cultural trainer Rachel Biale. "This healthy denial," she adds, "may be a response to the uncertainty of everyday life in Israel, or, on a deeper level, to their parents' helplessness in the face of the Holocaust."

But on the other side of the coin, survival in Israel has always meant reacting quickly and intelligently under pressure, both on and off the battlefield. Israelis make quick decisions and may have difficulty understanding why their international business partners process a decision to death while pondering twenty different options.

When the Iraqi Scud missiles were hitting Tel Aviv, the CEO of a Santa Clara, California telecommunications company feared that his joint venture partners in Tel Aviv would miss a crucial deadline. "Our Israeli engineers worked around-the-clock with their gas masks on," he said. "They're so phenomenal, they delivered the system component two weeks *before* the deadline." The American company was so happy with the results, it bought the Israeli company.

Business Meetings

It's important to figure out with whom you're dealing and how they work. Meetings, like Israelis, vary greatly. Some are quite formal and begin on the minute with military precision. In others, participants may wander in at different times and up to thirty minutes late. It may be difficult to tell who's in charge, especially when subordinates challenge the boss. And don't be surprised if the meeting frequently is interrupted — a daughter telephones, a secretary rushes in with papers to sign, a corporal announces he's back from military reserves.

Avoid Small Talk And Name Dropping

Israelis are generally inept at small talk. What some cultures consider to be social graces may seem superficial, insincere or artificially formal to Israelis. Don't bother commenting on the lovely weather or the view from your hotel. Israelis love the Yiddish word *tachles*, which means cutting through the verbiage and getting to down to business.

In your country, others may be impressed by your Harvard MBA or Oxford Ph.D; Israelis, however, are often more impressed by what you've accomplished in "the real world." An Israeli may be an MIT or Technion graduate, but that fact probably won't slip into the discussion. In business, goals and results are more important than titles. Israelis want to know if you're trustworthy, serious about doing business and able to deliver on your promises.

Why Bother With Icing? We'll Show You The Cake

In Israel, the product is much more important than the presentation. Some Israelis get suspicious if the icing is too sweet and thick — it may be hiding something. Don't be disappointed if the Israeli presentations are uneven, or if they lack elaborate brochures, slide shows or expensive video presentations. Many Israeli companies don't see the need for a hard sell approach. Their attitude may be, "Our product is the most technically advanced in the world. There's nothing like it on the market, so it'll sell itself. Why do we need a glossy brochure?" (This approach sometimes leads to headaches, the result of hastily written materials with English misspellings and bad grammar.)

Increasingly, however, Israeli companies with international affiliations are becoming sophisticated. They're learning the importance of marketing, sales, public relations and advertising. Some even have fancy brochures.

Forget About Finishing Your Sentences

If Israelis don't interrupt or ask questions, it could mean that you're not capturing their attention. If three or four Israelis talk at once, that's a good sign. The more interruptions, the better the meeting. If they get excited and speak loudly, they're probably quite interested. If someone starts pounding the table, you may be close to making a deal. Don't worry if they suddenly start arguing between themselves in Hebrew. They're not dealing behind your back. Israelis think faster and work better as a team in Hebrew. They'll translate after they reach a consensus.

Be Flexible

Israelis tend to be spontaneous (which can be good for creativity), so keep your agenda fluid. Be ready to change your plans as you receive new information. Let's say that your company has approved A, but during the meeting you find out the situation is B. If you take a long time to get new permission from your home office, Israelis may write you off as unresponsive and unable to make decisions.

Put It in Writing

Even Israelis fluent in English usually think in Hebrew (or Russian, or whatever their native tongue is) and then translate their ideas into English. So, your words may be interpreted differently from how you meant them. If you may say, "You should do X and Y," an Israeli might think, "Okay. That's your opinion. But I'll do what I want." To avoid crosscultural misunderstandings, make a verbal and/or written summary after every meeting. Flush out the issues and pinpoint what you've agreed and disagreed on. Then make clear exactly what you expect from each other.

As the business relationship progresses, trade informal memos, so you constantly understand where you agree. Convert these to formal documents only when all sides are ready to make a serious commitment of time and resources.

16 Negotiating with the Israelis

An Art Form

Israelis are experienced negotiators both in the boardroom and abroad. They've negotiated deals with an alphabet soup of different groups -- from the EU to the UN, to the PLO and the PRC (People's Republic of China). They're known for being tough but fair and have even been asked to help mediate foreign conflicts — between the Spanish government and the ETA (the Basque separatist group), for example, and between the Guatemalan government and the URNG guerrillas.

Many Israelis are multilingual; others hail from various parts of the globe. If the meeting is with English-language speakers, it will be conducted in English. However, if you wish to negotiate in Arabic, French, German, Russian, Spanish, Mandarin, etc., it's not difficult to find Israelis who can accommodate you.

Straight Talk = Talking Dugri

"Talking *dugri*" (an Arabic/Turkish word) means speaking bluntly, assertively, honestly and with a thorny *sabra* edge. When Israelis talk *dugri*, there's little posturing, subtlety or gamesmanship, and negotiations usually move quickly as a result. A positive aspect of talking *dugri* is that everyone knows where they stand. It can mean that an Israeli is showing you respect and thinks you have the strength and integrity to take frank, to-the-point talk. It can also mean that he thinks you want action, rather than empty words.

The New York Times recently quoted Israel's revered poet, Yehuda Amichai, as saying that "Jerusalem has no subconscious .... Everything is out in the open, even the infighting." Just substitute the word "Jerusalem" with "Israelis." This is talking *dugri* — the shooting-from-the-hip Israeli way.

Keep it Short and Simple

Israelis rarely soften their sentences with phrases like: "Perhaps you might consider..." or "If you wouldn't mind..." Instead, they'll say, "You're wrong!"

Israelis think in Hebrew, which is an extremely concise language. A three-word sentence may require eighteen words in French. A four-word Hebrew proverb may become sixteen words when translated into English. Israelis often speak English like they do Hebrew: tersely, economically and explicitly. Many English speakers love the eloquent speeches of former Israeli UN Ambassador Abba Eban. Many Israelis, however, criticize his rhetorical flair and "high sounding" language. If an Israeli observes that someone "doesn't speak like 'one of us,'" it isn't a compliment.

Assume They're A Few Steps Ahead

Israelis are adept at thinking strategically and anticipating what you might do next. That's why it's important to be even more prepared than you might think necessary. Don't let them surprise you. Anticipate in advance which angles might arise. Assume that the Israelis have already figured out your game plan and what they can get from you. If you feel that the negotiations are moving too rapidly, say that you need time to think. Don't be afraid to take a short break.

They'll test you, but if you're convinced you're right, be assertive and stand up for what you want. Speak *dugri* to them. Say, "These are the issues on your side and these are the ones on mine." Draw a line in the sand and stand firmly behind it. Israelis respect toughness. If they think you'll be a good partner, they'll probably compromise. If you're offering them a fair deal, they may be happy with a nice piece of a nice pie.

Finish the negotiations with a written agreement. Hire an experienced Israeli lawyer who knows your culture and your language. Beware of loopholes, but keep the agreement as short as possible. Most Israelis can't be bothered with forty-page contracts.

17 Business Outside the Law

According to a 1996 survey of businesspeople from 54 countries conducted by Germany's Gottingen University, Israel ranks fourth as the least corrupt country in which to conduct business. (The United States ranks fifth.)

Drug Trafficking

The same peace process that now makes it easier for former enemies to work together also makes it easier for Israeli and Arab smugglers to ply their trade. Over the past decade, drug trafficking in Israel has shot up about 2,000 percent. About 95 percent of drug shipments go uncaught by understaffed and underfunded Israeli police squads.

Most of it is heroin from Syrian-controlled Lebanon, where the drug trade is a multi-billion dollar business. Lebanese and Syrian drug lords and army officials oversee poppy fields in the Bekaa Valley, where Interpol sources estimate that about l00 drug labs transform the flowers' bitter, brownish juice into a potent narcotic. Lebanon also is a key switching point for heroin, cocaine and hashish shipments originating in Turkey, Iran, South America, India,

Afghanistan, and Pakistan — destined for European and North American markets. As drug transfers are less likely to be intercepted when sent through Israel, Arabs have formed partnerships with Israeli smugglers. Sometime smugglers enter with the few thousand Lebanese who legally cross the Israeli border daily to work. Most drugs just transit through Israel; fewer than 0.3 percent of Israelis use them, and only five percent of those 18 years of age and under have ever even tried drugs (compared to 50 percent of that same age group in the U.S.).

Anti-drug surveillance at Israel's entry points is getting tighter and more officials are undergoing anti-drug training and using sniffer dogs. Recently, Israeli port officials intercepted a container ship filled with hashish from Bombay.

But Israeli officials are much more preoccupied with security. Vehicles crossing the border from Egypt, Jordan, Lebanon and the Palestinian Authority are searched for weapons and explosives, not drugs. Although Egyptian authorities are working much harder than their Lebanese counterparts, smugglers continue to slip across the largely unguarded Sinai border with Israel.

The Organizatsiya

Israeli officials have little experience with large-scale organized crime. Like Europeans and North Americans, they're unprepared for the ruthless *Organizatsiya* (Russian Mafia), which is heavily involved in international drugs, prostitution, extortion and theft. Until recently, Israel's liberal foreign currency rules and banking regulations (drawn up to help new immigrants) attracted corrupt former Communist party and KGB officials who "laundered" money in Israel and then transferred the funds electronically to fellow Russians in the West. Israeli banks eventually caught on and no longer allow major deposits from Russian foreign currency reserves. Only a handful of these mobsters are Jewish immigrants in Israel. Most, according to Israeli officials working closely with Russian police, are non-Jewish Russians living abroad.

Taxi Drivers

Unless you tell them, taxi drivers often won't put on their meters. Play it legal and insist that they do. A driver may try to convince you ("It's cheaper if I don't use my meter, okay?") If you want to sharpen your negotiating skills, try bargaining. But first find out the official meter charge: ask your hotel concierge, call the taxi company, or consult the taxi's official rate book. And be aware of the fact that drivers can spot a virgin bargainer. If you're skilled, you and the driver may end up splitting the difference on the meter price. During your ride, he'll probably talk non-stop, giving you his opinions about everything, especially politics. In Israel, the taxi drivers even started their own political party!

Stolen Cars

The recent "peace dividend" with the Palestinians has brought with it a dividend of another sort. Israeli police have been unable to stop a serious wave of car-thefts — in 1995, over 35,000 vehicles were stolen. With 25 thefts per 1,000 cars, Israel has a higher rate than any western European country. Most end up in the West Bank and Gaza and are openly driven around. Recently, a Palestinian official drove a new Volvo to a meeting. His Israeli counterpart recognized the car as the very one that had been stolen from him a few days before.

18 Titles & Status

First-Name Basis

The egalitarianism of Israel's socialist founders encouraged people of all stripes — employers and employees, schoolchildren and teachers — to interact on a first-name basis. The former Mayor of Jerusalem is referred to by all as Teddy, not Mr. Kollek. Golda Meir was Golda, not Mrs. Prime Minister. Waiters, hotel clerks, bellhops and taxi drivers treat visitors "just like everybody else." In this land of rampant informality, most people are treated with an equal lack of deference.

Even in the IDF, soldiers show little respect for rank. Privates and generals call each other by first names. What's important is to be one of the *hevreh* (the group). After the army, however, service in an elite unit like the paratroopers often carries more weight than an engineering degree from the Technion. Ex-generals and war heroes (some of whom may have flunked out of the Technion) have a great advantage when it comes to securing key jobs in the public sector. A number of war heroes, such as Generals Moshe Dayan and Itzhak Rabin, decided to continue their fighting careers on the political battlefield.

As more and more Israelis enter the global business arena, they're becoming aware that most cultures are far more title and status-conscious than they are. Sometimes, it's a shock. "A few years ago, on my first trip to New York, I asked a young woman at an advertising agency if she was the secretary," said the founder of an educational software firm. "She glared at my sandals and informed me, in a huffy tone, that she is an 'account executive.' I couldn't stop laughing. Americans make such a big deal about titles." The next year, however, after a business trip (*sans* sandals) to London and Tokyo, he stopped laughing. "My Japanese business associates didn't know how deeply to bow until they'd studied my business card. I'd had engraved ones printed up and I'd given myself a big shot title — president and chief executive officer and Ph.D. They bowed very deeply."

The New Materialism

As the economic gap widens, Israel's egalitarian legacy is weakening. For years, bus drivers earned more than doctors. In the 1970s, many Israelis earned about the same salary: $300–400 a month; today, a software engineer can earn over ten times that. Society frowned on materialism so much that the few affluent Israelis were reluctant to display their wealth. Today, *shekel*-laden Israelis are flaunting their newly found affluence — moving into glass and chrome offices, driving new BMWs, wearing designer sun glasses and eating tofu burgers in trendy bistros.

But the government is another story. Some government jobs may come with prestigious titles, but not the big salaries or state-of-the-art offices to match. The mayor of Jerusalem (Ehud Olmert) earns only $24,000 annually. Former ambassadors who work for Jerusalem's Foreign Ministry spend their days in cramped offices in a dilapidated former army barracks. Only the Director General's unpretentious office has air conditioning. However, in 1998, when the Foreign Ministry moves into a new building, all offices will have air conditioning. Israel's socialist founding fathers and mothers would probably be shocked.

M.D., Ing., Ms.

Academic titles and degrees (such as M.D. and PhD.) are used by businesspeople. The European-style Ing. (Engineer) is used in Hebrew. The appropriate address for women is Ms., because in Hebrew, *geveret* is the form of address for both married and unmarried women.

"SLOW DOWN!"   "OH NO!"   "YESSS!"

19 Communication Styles

With so many high volume conversations, few Israelis need hearing aids. As you've read, Israelis love to debate and negotiate. They thrive on confrontations. If you see someone arguing and then exploding, it's probably just a healthy discussion. He or she will probably calm down quickly. Just watch and enjoy the show.

Israelis are often quite humorous. Sometimes, however, outsiders misunderstand their sarcastic edge. For example, when an American told her Israeli friend. "I'll call you soon," the Israeli answered: "Don't threaten me." The American was offended. History has taught Israelis to inject cynical or black humor into extremely grave situations, especially following a war or terrorist attack. After the recent spate of bus bombings, the monthly "free pass" bus ticket (you pay for a month's worth of rides and get one ride free) was dubbed "Free — to Heaven."

Body Language

Many Israelis express themselves with their shoulders, their hands and their faces. They can laugh with their entire bodies or undress you with only their eyes. When Israelis speak, they often stand close together and touch each other to make sure they're being understood or listened to, or to emphasize a point. It's difficult for an Israeli to express a profusion of ideas without gesturing. In an experiment, when Israelis were instructed to sit on their hands, they couldn't articulate their thoughts clearly.

Common Nonverbal Expressions

Sounds and nonverbal expressions you may encounter include:

- Tsk.
  Instead of saying "no," Israelis make a loud "tsk" sound with their tongues. (This can also indicate disapproval or impatience.)
  Here's a conversation with a secretary.
  "Is Mr. Gur here yet?"
  "Tsk."
  "Do you know when he's expected?"
  "Tsk."

- Ech? Ech?
  This means "What?" or "I don't understand."

- Nu?
  With different inflections, this Yiddish word can mean almost anything. For example: Nu? as in "How are you?" Nu??? as in "You expect me to do everything at once?" Or nuuuu????? as in "You're impatient because the line is too slow."

- To indicate "Slow down" or "Wait a minute":
  Raise your right hand, palm upward. Touch the tips of your fingers together and move your hand back and forth.

- To indicate "Oh no!" or "Now what?":
  Put hands on your head, then lift your shoul-

ders in a shrug.

- To indicate "Wow!":
  Smack your lips and say, "Ooo-wah."

- To indicate "Come here":
  Put your right palm up, then open and close it.

- To indicate "Go away":
  Put your right palm down, then move it as if shooing a fly.

- To indicate "Great!" or "Yesss!":
  Make your right hand into a fist, with the thumb pointing upward.

20 Customs

Visiting A Synagogue

Jews believe that God is present everywhere. It doesn't matter whether the synagogue (a Jewish house of prayer) is ornate or a bare room. Most Israeli synagogues are Orthodox, which means that men and women sit separately, so as not to distract each other.

Heads are covered in deference to God. Married Orthodox women wear scarves, hats or wigs (a few still shave their heads, according to a tradition that would not have them be attractive to men other than their husbands); men wear *kipot* (yarmulkes or skullcaps). Men also strap *tefillin* (two black boxes with prayers inside) onto their forehead and on the hand. Women wear dresses or skirts with modest blouses that cover their shoulders.

All synagogues have a Holy Ark (which faces the Temple Mount in Jerusalem) that contains at least one handwritten *Torah* scroll. The *Torah* contains the first five books of Moses: *Genesis, Exodus, Leviticus, Numbers* and *Deuteronomy.* This sacred document describes events from the creation of the world to the death of Moses and prescribes rituals, holy days, morals and laws. Services are led either by a rabbi (Hebrew for "teacher of traditions") or a learned layperson. Remember, when greeting very Orthodox Jews, that they're not allowed to touch people of the opposite sex.

Visiting A Mosque

Unless you're a Moslem (literally "those who submit to God"), you must ask permission to enter a mosque. (Non-Moslems may not enter during sermons or prayers.) Many Moslems perform a ritual washing outside; all remove their shoes before entering. Women should dress modestly, with shoulders and legs covered.

Orthodox Moslems pray prostrate five times a day facing Mecca in Saudi Arabia — a *mihrab* or niche in the mosque wall indicates the direction. Like the Jews, the Moslems are monotheistic, and the *Koran* is their Book of God. Men and women pray separately. Services are performed by an *imam*. On Friday, the traditional Moslem day of rest, the *imam* usually gives a public sermon.

Kashrut: Jewish Dietary Laws

A cultural glue for over 2000 years, the laws of *kashrut* designate which foods Jews may eat and how they should be prepared. These dietary guidelines are described in detail in *Deuteronomy*, one of the five books of Moses, written circa 1275 B.C.E. Many Israeli Jewish families eat only foods that are *kosher* (fit or proper) and not foods that are *trafe* (forbidden). What does this mean?

- Forget the ham sandwich. Why? Only animals that chew their cud and have split hooves are kosher. Sheep, oxen, goats and antelope are fine, but pigs, horses, camels and donkeys aren't.

- Forget the seafood salad with clams, crabs, shrimp, lobster and mussels. Why? Shellfish and fish without fins and scales are forbidden.

- Forget the veal Parmesan or a cheeseburger. Why? Milk and meat are never served together. In Exodus, it's written, "Thou shall not cook a kid (baby goat) in its mother's milk," possibly because this was a pagan custom. Meat and milk products must be kept as separate as possible; kosher kitchens have two separate sets of utensils and dishware for dairy and meat meals.

- All kosher meat or poultry must come from animals killed in a traditional way (swiftly, with a minimum of suffering to the animal, and so that all the blood is drained) by a licensed *shochet* (kosher slaughterer).

Jewish Holidays

Holidays are important to Israelis, whether they are religious or not. The year is a round of sacred occasions, gay or somber. Holidays (including the Sabbath) always begin just before sunset on the evening before, and end just after sunset (when the first three stars appear) on the day of the holiday. Here are four of the most important ones:

Shabbat (also known as the Sabbath). This is the most important day in the Jewish calendar. It's a time for reflection, conversation and rest. Jewish businesses close, buses stop running (except in Haifa) and El Al, the national airline, is grounded. For the Orthodox (16 percent of Israel's Jews), "rest" means no telephoning, writing, cooking, driving or surfing the Internet. But most Israelis are not Orthodox. They celebrate Shabbat as a vacation from the demands of the week, a day for visiting with friends and family.

Shabbat honors the Creation (Genesis: "God created the world in six days and then rested on the seventh day"), follows the dictate of one of the Ten Commandments ("Remember the Sabbath day and keep it holy"), and serves to bind people together. As the Talmud (the Rabbinic interpretation of the Torah) states, "More than that Israel has kept the Sabbath, the Sabbath has kept the people of Israel."

The holiday begins every Friday evening at home, with the lighting of at least two candles and the reciting of a blessing — thus marking the transition from secular to sacred time. (Friday night candlelighting dates back to the first century B.C.E.) Blessings over wine and bread (except during Passover) follow, and there's often a festive meal with guests. Ancient rabbis compared the Sabbath to a bride and its celebration to a wedding.

Rosh Hashanah (literally, "beginning of the year"). Along with Yom Kippur, it's considered a "high holy day," a time for intense prayer and reflection. The blowing of a *shofar* (a ram's horn, one of the world's oldest instruments) celebrates God as the creator and reminds Jews to right the wrongs they've committed during the past year. During the "Ten Days of Repentance" (beginning with Rosh Hashanah and culminating ten days later on Yom Kippur), God decides peoples' fates for the coming year.

Yom Kippur (also known as Day of Atonement or the Day of Judgment). Jews gather in synagogues to scrutinize their lives and seek forgiveness for their transgressions against God. (Sins against people can be forgiven only by those who were sinned against.) Observant Jews fast from sundown to sundown, so they can focus fully on spiritual matters. It's the only day of the year when travel ceases completely; airports, hotels, restaurants and all Jewish businesses close. As the stars appear, one long blast of the *shofar* heralds the end of the day, and Jews celebrate with a break-the-fast meal.

Pesah (Passover). This week-long celebration commemorates the end of 400 years of slavery under the Egyptian pharaohs. By extension, it reminds Jews of the need to battle for freedom for all peoples. During Passover, no leavened foods (breads and other products that contain yeast) are consumed. Instead, Jews eat *matza* or unleavened bread, in memory of the ancient Israelites' hasty flight from Egypt — when there had been no time for that day's dough to rise and it baked, instead, under the desert sun. Families celebrate with a *seder*, a special dinner during which the story of Moses leading his people toward the Promised Land is recounted. An array of symbolic foods are eaten, including *charosis* (a mixture of chopped apples and nuts that resembles mortar, in memory of the Hebrews' forced labor). It's also traditional to lean on pillows during the meal — in ancient times, the symbol of a free man's table.

21 Dress & Appearance

Until recently, formal dress for an Israeli man meant a clean shirt, new jeans and sneakers (instead of sandals). Partially because of the country's social-ist-egalitarian past (when neckties were forbidden), clothes were for covering up or keeping warm. Presidents worked in open-necked shirts; Prime Minister Golda Meir dressed like a frumpy grandmother and sometimes held cabinet meetings in her kitchen. For many Israelis, "style" ranges from informal to very informal. In the 1960s and 70s, diplomats from some countries sent invitations that read *Tenue Israelienne* ("Israeli dress"), that is, very casual and no ties for men.

Even at a funeral, it's still rare to see men in jackets or ties, or women in suits. In the late 1970s, however, the Likud party did the unthinkable: it made jackets and ties symbolic of capitalism, in order to set themselves apart from the socialist Labor Party. Then, in the late 1980s, the young, well-dressed technocrats of the Labor Party became known as "the Blazers," because they dressed like American yuppies.

Today, even some kibbutzniks are doing what was previously unthinkable. "I recently did something ridiculous," recalls a 44-year-old. "I wore a suit and tie for the first time when I went to Europe and Japan to sell *koi* (expensive carp for decorative ponds). Luckily, no one on the kibbutz saw me. I looked like a penguin."

Israelis no longer snicker at suit-and-tie-clad lawyers, government officials and Knesset members. Former Prime Minister Shimon Peres is an elegant dresser who usually removed his tie only when visiting the troops. Men may wear sports jackets (and sometimes ties) when meeting international visitors. Women wear everything from ultra-casual to stylish dresses or slacks. When the heat goes up, their clothes may get skimpy, or what some Orthodox Jews call "provocative." (Orthodox women cover their arms and heads and wear long skirts to cover their legs, regardless of the temperature). There's a growing fashion trendiness, especially among the young, who watch *Beverly Hills 90210* and *MTV* and shop at the Gap.

In sum, there are no real dress codes. An Israeli man or woman in shorts and sandals could still be a mayor, a leading scientist, or high-tech millionaire. When conducting business, dress comfortably and more casually than you would back home — but not so casually that you'll seem like you're trying to out-Israeli the Israelis.

Traditional Arab Attire

Some men may wear *kaffiyeh* (a square of cloth folded to form a triangle and held on with a cord; named for the Iraqi town of Al Kufa). Many traditional women wear long dresses and cover their heads with scarfs. However, it's increasing difficult to tell many younger, nontraditional Israeli Arabs and Israeli Jews apart.

22 Entertaining

Eating in an Israeli Jewish or Arab Home

After a business meeting, don't expect to spend the evening alone in your hotel room. Israelis take care of visitors, and they enjoy entertaining in their houses and apartments. When Israelis say "Drop by," they mean it. They're very family oriented, so spouses and children are usually welcome. Don't be insulted if the invitation is extended "at the last minute." Israelis tend to be spontaneous. If you're told that dinner will be at 9 P.M., ask your host in a light-hearted manner, "Israeli or Western time?" (Israelis tend to arrive late.) Whatever time you do get there, Israeli guests will probably arrive later. And don't be surprised if they bring uninvited friends.

Lunch is usually the biggest meal of the day. If you're invited to an Arab house for lunch at 2 P.M., you might arrive early so you can socialize. This shows your host you're not there only to eat.

It's gracious to bring a gift such as fancy chocolates, flowers or wine. (Avoid the latter if your hosts are Moslem. Islam prohibits the drinking of alcoholic beverages.) If you know your host, ask what gift you might bring *before* you arrive in Israel.

Israelis are not shy about such questions. Since many Western products are heavily taxed here, popular requests may include good books, cosmetics, electronic gadgets or children's' clothes.

Most Israelis are not heavy drinkers — they can nurse a bottle of beer or glass of wine all night. A common toast is *l'chayim* ("to life"). People often smoke in homes without asking permission. If the smoke bothers you, it's acceptable to ask, "Please, would you mind?" Whether you're eating in an Israeli Arab or a Jewish home, you're guaranteed to be plied with food until you fall into a coma. So, when your stomach finally rebels, compliment your host profusely, *insist* that you're truly full, and then ask for a recipe.

When visiting an Arab Israeli family, say, "*Halas, shokran*" (enough, thanks). Many Moslems, like many Jews, abstain from eating pork. When dining with Arabs, never use your left hand (it's associated with personal hygiene and therefore considered unclean).

In both Jewish and Arab homes, you may be invited just for a evening coffee, along with an assortment of cakes and cookies (or something more elaborate). If you're lucky, you'll get to sample the best sweet in the Middle East — warm, cheese-filled *kanafeh*. If you're offered a tray with mint tea or very sweet, thick Turkish coffee in tiny cups, be prepared for puzzled looks if you don't take sugar.

Israelis rarely set a time for a party or evening to end. The longer guests stay, the better the party and the happier the host. Afterward, don't call or send a thank you note. Israelis find such customs oddly formal and phony. If you're enjoying yourself, show it. Stay late.

Restaurant Revolution

Until recently, Israel was a culinary backwater. Dining out meant eating falafel, drinking Maccabee beer, or eating one of two cuts of meat — slices or chunks. The Foreign Ministry even resorted to giving young recruits crash courses in etiquette — including how to eat a meal with three different forks and how to mix a Bloody Mary.

But in the 1990s, a "gourmet revolution" brought an explosion of fine restaurants, from Chinese to Russian to Indian. You can order Indonesian *rijstafel* or *sushi* prepared by the world's first Yemenite-Lithuanian-Israeli sushi chef.

If you're watching your budget, try Middle Eastern *shishlick* (skewered meat), North African *couscous* (often served with a stew of lamb or seafood), or *burekas*, a warm, stuffed pastry native to Bulgaria. "White steak" on a menu is a euphemism for pork.

Rules of the Game

If an Israeli says, "Let's meet for dinner at ten tonight," don't be surprised. Israelis often sit down to dine between 8 and 11 P.M., stay out late, and still manage to show up for work the next day.

You'll notice that wherever Israelis go, they run into buddies. If your host spots friends, he may stop to talk to them without introducing you, or invite them to join your table. If the conversation gets exciting, Israelis may switch unconsciously from English to Hebrew. Don't be shy about speaking up. Try some guilt. Say, "This sounds so interesting. Too bad I can't understand." When Israelis socialize, they tend to forget the clock. Waiters won't rush you or bring the check unless asked. Bills don't usually include a service charge. Tips are 12 to 15 percent.

23 Socializing

Night Life Ends at Dawn

Israel's motto in the 1990s seems to be: Life is uncertain, so eat dessert first.

Maybe that explains the packed outdoor cafes. Politicians and journalists have their favorite haunts, as do artists and students. Trendy discos are crammed with tourists and soldiers alike; some feature Latin jazz, others play African or Israeli music or techno rock. Some Israelis take afternoon naps, so they can be re-energized for the night life, which usually doesn't begin until after 10 P.M. and can last until sunrise

Tel Aviv is a city that never sleeps. Wednesdays and Thursdays are big hang-out nights for locals. Friday and Saturday nights, the city fills with soldiers on leave and people who live out of town (what New Yorkers would call "the bridge and tunnel crowd"). There are designer coffee bars and pubs for everyone from yuppies to Embassy types. Some nightclubs cater to karaoke singers, others attract "swinging singles." One club has a telephone at each table. If you see someone you fancy, you can call for a dance.

A Passion For The Land

Israelis love to show off their country to guests. You might be invited on hikes, taught the names of flowers or be shown Biblical and archaeological sites. On Shabbat, car trips may last longer than expected, as the roads are one giant traffic jam. Because the country is so small, you're never far from a beach. And because Israelis are aware of the dangers of the sun, there's a massive onslaught in the early morning hours and between 5 and 9 P.M.

Music and Dance

Israel has the world's largest number of concert musicians per capita. Yitzhak Perlman, Pinhas Zukerman and Daniel Barenboim received their training here and return regularly to perform. The influx of Russian immigrants has led to the creation of many excellent small orchestras (as well as Israel's Philharmonic). Russian street musicians who sound as if they belong on the concert stage probably once did.

Immigrant musicians — from Ethiopia to Yemen — add to the multi-cultural feast. Music festivals are held all over the country all year long. Don't miss the New Israeli Opera, or concerts by Israel's Achinoam Nini, beloved singer/composer Arik Einstein, or hot pop stars Rita and Yehudit Ravitz. Middle Eastern music is also popular.

There's The Israel Ballet, spectacular folk dance groups like the Inbal (Yemenite), or the modern Batsheva and Bat Dor dance companies. *Kol Demama* (Voice of Silence) is an unusual group of deaf and hearing-impaired dancers who "hear" the vibrations through their feet.

Basic Phrases

English	Hebrew
hello/ good-bye/peace	*shalom*
good morning	*boker tov*
good evening	*erev tov*
yes	*ken*
no	*lo*
ok	*beseder*
good	*tov*
bad	*ra*
thank you	*to-dah* or *todah raba*
excuse me	*sli-ha*
please/you're welcome	*be-va-ka-shah*
where? or where is?	*ai-fo?*
how much is it?	*ka-ma-zeh?*
see you later	*ley-hit-ra-ot*
bill	*heshbon*
what?	*ma?*
post office	*do-ar*
right	*yamin*

English	Hebrew
left	*smol*
when?	*matai?*
good luck (we signed the deal)	*mazal tov*

Arabic

English	Arabic
hello	*mar-ha-ba, a-halen*
good-bye	*ma'a salaama*
yes	*aiwa*
no	*la*
good	*ka-why-is*
please thank you	*min fadlack* *shokran*
welcome	*ahlan wa sahlan*
thank god	*hamdu lillah*
god willing	*inshallah*
let's go	*yahllah*
how much?	*adeish?*
how are you? (to man) (to woman)	*keefahk* *keefek?*
some days are better than others (days of honey, days of onion)	*yom asal, yom basal*
pardon?	*sa-mach-nee?*
when?	*emtah?*
where?	*fean?*
right	*yemin*
left	*shmal*

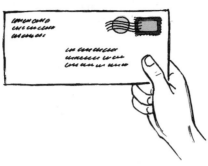

 ## Correspondence

The order of information in an Israeli address is the same as in the West. For example:

Nir Shaler
64 Druyanov Street
63143 Tel Aviv
Israel

Sometimes, the spelling of translated Hebrew and Arabic words vary. For example, house (bet or beit); street (rehov or re'khov); road (derek or de'rekh); avenue or boulevard (sderot or sde'rot); and square (kikar or ki'kar).

Company names are often translated into English. Mo'tsi'im La'or Ben'leumi B.M. might become International Publishers Ltd.

Israel uses a five-digit postal code, which should precede the city name.

European-style dates are used in correspondence. For example: 6 January 1997 or 6.1.97.

26 Useful Numbers

These are local Israeli numbers. If dialing from outside Israel, dial your country's international access code, then Israel's country code [972]. Israel has 7 area codes: north (06), Haifa (04), Tel Aviv (03), Herzylia and the Sharon (09), Shfela (08), Jerusalem and surrounding areas (02), and the south, including Eilat, (07). (In 1997-1998, Israel will be switching to a one-area-code system.)

For English-language phone listings, use *The Golden Book*.

- International Access Code 00
- Police 100
- Ambulance (Magen David Adom) 101
- Fire 102
- Information (English speaking operators) 144
- Overseas Operator 188
- Collect Local Calls 142
- Flight arrivals and departures (in English)
  .... (03) 972-3344
- Israel Export Institute .... (03) 514-2830
- Ministry of Industry and Trade .... (02) 220220
- Ministry of Finance .... (02) 317-1111884
- Israel Business Today magazine ..... (03) 639-7194
- Tel Aviv Stock Exchange .... (03) 567-7405

Publications & Internet Addresses

30 Opportunities for Your Company to Do Business Successfully In Israel by Elmer Winter. Committee for Economic Growth of Israel, USA. (Free.) Tel: 414. 961-1000 Fax: 414-963-4171

Crossing Boundaries: American Interactions with Israelis by Lucy Shahar and David Kurtz, Intercultural Press, Yarmouth, Maine, USA, 1995. Common cultural communication problems and useful coping strategies.

The Jerusalem Report, the best English language source for news and commentary on Israel (biweekly magazine).
Subscriptions: U.S. and Canada 1-800-827-1119
POB 1805; 91017 Jerusalem, Israel
Fax: 02-291-037

Link Magazine (Israeli business & technology)
Israeli fax: 03-537-4073

Internet Addresses

Globes (Israel's financial newspaper)
http://www.globes.co.il

Jerusalem Post (daily or weekly newspaper)
http://www.jpost.co.il

Israel Business Today (biweekly newsletter).
Subscriptions — CompuServe:100274,570

The Federation of Israeli Chambers of Commerce
http://www.chamber.org.il

Israel Ministry of Finance
http://ww.macom.co.il/Government/MOF/

Israeli Internet Center (lists over 30 web sites)
http://www.macom.cc.il

Ministry of Industry and Trade
http://www.cbp.gov.il

Israel Investor Network
http://www.iin18.com/

Israel Trade & Investment
http://www.std.com/neicc/

Israel Export Institute
amcohen@export.gov.il.

Israeli Internet Center (lists over 30 web sites)
http://www.macom.cc.il

American-Israeli Chambers of Commerce
http://www.std.com.neicc/anaicci.html

Israel Economic Mission to North America
(includes hypertext references to all sites dealing with business & economics)
http://www.iin18.com/iem/

Israel Investor Network
http://www